From Daydream to Dream Job

Don't like the cover
reminded me of
Soviet times, & kind
of bloody news of
torture deals
& creative people dreams
who in prison the beast
that the rest of
us cannot.

From Daydream to Dream Job

Make Money Being Creative

Raia King, MBA

LONDON MEDIA
PUBLISHING

From Daydream to Dream Job: Make Money Being Creative

London Media Publishing
P.O. Box 1422
Exton, PA 19341

FIRST EDITION

Library of Congress Control Number: 2011917460

ISBN 978-0-9846954-0-9

Cover designed by Mark King
Photos by Raia King and Karen A. R. Pannepacker

Published by London Media Publishing, Exton, Pennsylvania
June 9, 2012 (4)

To the love of my life, Mark,
and to my wonderful parents

Table of Contents

- wedding professionals (Engage!)

Preface

I have seen many creative entrepreneurs needlessly sign away rights to their work or sell themselves short to try to become successful. The price for following your heart doesn't have to be selling your soul in business.

For years I have taught marketing classes to people in all sorts of professions. While I enjoy working with entrepreneurs of all types, I have a particular affinity for creative entrepreneurs because I can appreciate the distinct business challenges they face.

I come from a very creative family, so I am happiest when immersed in creativity. My family includes generations of painters, photographers, and crafters. My mother is a costume designer and a former QVC stylist. My father always did all kinds of beautiful woodwork in every house in which we lived. My brother was a DJ, my sister and I were singers in rock bands when we were younger, and I'm a writer and former songwriter. My life was filled with creative influences, so I grew up thinking that the same was true for everyone else. From where I stood in life, I got the impression that most people were creative.

I'll never forget being in a class at university and hearing the professor ask, "How many people here have been told they're not creative?" I distinctly recall thinking that was a silly question because surely not many people would raise their hands. To my surprise, a *majority* of my classmates raised their hands. I knew not everyone was creative, but I never expected that response! Next, the professor asked students to picture specific images in their minds and asked how many people were unable to do it. Again I saw that many people had difficulty with what I thought was effortless for most people. It dawned on me that such a difference has far-reaching repercussions in business when a creative person is working with a non-creative person. They could be working on the same project yet literally have completely different views on that project.

I'm certainly not saying that one type of ability is better than another because we *all* have different gifts and they're *all* important, but what I am saying is that I have seen anecdotally that these differences do matter in a business setting. Someone who can't imagine something they've never seen or encountered before can understandably have difficulty imagining a business endeavor that a creative person can see as clearly as if it already exists. This is a significant difference that is important to recognize. Simply having an awareness of this can defuse many a tense business situation and help you avoid taking some people's opinions personally.

As a creative entrepreneur you need to remain strong because it can be a tough road. Fortunately, the rewards are well worth the journey.

What's the difference between a hobby and a profession? Revenue. You *can* make money in a creative job, but you need a plan to become successful. With the right planning, marketing tools, and talent you *can* turn your passion into a profession.

My goal in writing this book is to offer creative entrepreneurs (e.g. musicians, artists, crafters, photographers, woodworkers, comedians, writers, wedding planners, etc.) practical business tools, encouragement, and emotional support. I know what you're going through, and I have experienced years of frustration going through the same types of challenges you face now.

In this book, I have tried to provide the kind of marketing information that can help creative entrepreneurs get started on the right track. In my experience one of the biggest challenges for creative people trying to become profitable is developing a solid business model that can generate income. Creative entrepreneurs often face difficulty in defining exactly how to get to where they want to be in business. This is one of the most important steps in achieving profitability in a creative field. The marketing tools and advice on the pages that follow can help you turn an enjoyable hobby into a profitable profession.

Certainly one book can't provide the innumerable aspects of marketing. Such a tome would be voluminous beyond reason. Instead, I chose to address the issues that you will encounter most frequently as you begin the process without overwhelming you with information.

As you continue on your journey toward success, it is wise to read books about marketing and business. In the future I'll be releasing more books addressing various business matters in further detail, but be sure to read books from many different sources. Network with other entrepreneurs and learn from each other. Visit websites that offer articles about business and marketing to gain even more information. Everything you learn can help you succeed, so try to learn as much as you can.

I am a firm believer that knowledge is power. The more information you have, the better able you will be to make wise decisions. You will feel stronger in negotiating situations where thousands or even millions of dollars may be at stake. Learning is just like going to the gym, only for your mind instead of your body. It makes you stronger and more powerful. It enables you to achieve bigger and better things and make your business dreams a reality. Never underestimate the power that knowledge can give you.

Study your industry and know your worth so you can build your career on *your* terms instead of someone else's. With the right business tools, a lot of dedication, great ideas, and plenty of hard work, you can start making money doing what you love.

Raia King

Acknowledgments

There are so many people who helped me in various ways to bring this book to market. I am grateful to all of them.

I thank my husband, Mark King, who encouraged me through countless late-night writing sessions. His love and support through this process have kept me motivated and meant the world to me.

To my parents, Frederick D. and Jeanette Rotar, I have immeasurable gratitude. They gave me a huge head start in life by teaching me to read at a very young age and by exemplifying a strong work ethic.

Tremendous thanks to Eric F. Rotar and Karen A. R. Pannepacker for their endless encouragement.

Thanks to Martha Bullen for her generous advice, wisdom, and professional guidance throughout this process.

Thanks to David Yeager for doing such a detailed and stellar job proofreading the manuscript.

I am grateful to Rick Gillis for his honesty, time, and savvy suggestions when I needed another perspective.

Thanks to Danette Kubanda for her professional insight, which has expanded my marketing horizons.

Thanks to Bill Harrison and Steve Harrison for being such inspirational entrepreneurs and for their promotional help.

Many thanks go to Jolee Land, Scott E. Scioli, Esq., Shawn Edgington, Cameron Munson, Gail Snyder, Rose Glotfelty, Pamela Oatham, John Gay, Tom Lowe, Brad Trout, Mitch Selko, Wendy Lipton-Dibner, M.A., Hal Dibner, Ph.D., Richard Hudson, and Erica House for their valuable feedback and promotional help.

it feels surreal to know the people in the acknowledgments

Disclaimer

The information contained in this book is for general informational purposes only and should not be viewed as legal advice or financial advice and neither the publisher nor the author will be held liable in any way for its use. When legal, financial, or other advice is required, you should consult a qualified professional to obtain advice that pertains to your specific situation and needs. While the publisher and author have made every reasonable effort to ensure all information in this book is correct, there may be mistakes within this book so it should be used only as a general source of information.

No amount of information can guarantee success or profitability. The information must be used in a judicious manner to be effective. The publisher and the author accept no responsibility for any individual's or organization's business outcomes as a result of following the advice in this book. Readers are encouraged to use common sense and discretion while using any information in this book.

visualisation
helps you emotionally
put one (in) needs to
do the work to succeed

people believe they
have one shot, the caman (sic)
gene, Herches failed
# of times before
reaching success.

CHAPTER 1

There Are No Secrets to Success

The True Cause of Success

We live in an age of televised talent shows and reality TV programs that make people celebrities overnight. What perpetually surprises me, however, is how frequently the contestants on these programs say that if they don't win these televised competitions, they'll never make it in the entertainment business. Fortunately for them, nothing could be further from the truth.

It's a big world out there, and people have been able to attain success long before reality TV became, well . . . a reality. If you have the talent and skills for the job and can get your message out to enough people, you can work in any creative field.

> **There is no magic to success and no talisman that can ensure prosperity.**

I'm well aware of the popular belief that people can gain financial prosperity by simply thinking about what they want. Having studied the workings of business in depth when I earned my MBA, I just can't view business in a mystical way. There is no magic to success and no talisman that can ensure prosperity.

In the cases when I have seen multimillionaires cite this as the reason for their success, what I typically find is simply that they are attributing the results of their hard work to something other than their own effort. They're giving credit to their thoughts instead of their actions. They should give themselves the credit, since they worked so hard to earn it!

Imagine asking your investment manager what strategy was being used to build your retirement funds and being told, "I'm thinking positive thoughts." Would you leave your funds with that person or move them?

I have often heard those who subscribe to this theory say that as they began to think differently about success, they began to achieve success. Invariably, however, as they explain in detail how they became more successful, I hear them talking about concrete marketing practices, such as networking and business development. They often didn't do these things before simply because they didn't know about them. There is no magic to these practices, anyone can learn them and anyone can do them. They are as old as business itself and can easily be found in thousands of marketing books.

In fact, I'll address these in detail later in this book. My point is that anyone can do these things, but they require one essential element: hard work. No amount of wishing or attitude adjustment will make things happen for you. You have to get out there in the world and make them happen for yourself.

Because there is no magic to achieving success, it's important to learn business skills. There are simple business tools and processes out there that anyone can use if they learn how to use them effectively. I have heard many motivational speakers claim that achieving success is all in a person's attitude, but that simply isn't true. There are thousands, perhaps millions, of people out there who have terrific attitudes but aren't bringing in any business revenue. They have great intentions and big dreams but, without taking the correct action, being tenacious, and working hard, their aspirations will most likely remain nothing more than just dreams.

Once people begin to gain some ground in their pursuit of success, they will also begin to gain more wealth in the process. At that point, there will be business resources available that were previously unavailable to them because they lacked sufficient funding to pay for these resources. Again, this has nothing to do with thinking your way to success, it simply has to do with the ability to afford resources to bring about growth in a business. Money opens doors and makes things happen more quickly because financial resources can be used to pay experts who can quickly advance a person's career or business. If achieving success were as easy as simply envisioning the desired success, wouldn't we all be tremendously successful? Of course we would.

The truth about achieving success is that hard work, skill, and perseverance can help you achieve success. It may sound old fashioned, and it's certainly not glamorous, but it's the plain truth. You don't need any mystical direction or esoteric information to succeed. All you need to do is educate yourself in some fashion, whether it's through taking classes, reading pertinent books and articles, or speaking to experts in the field you want to enter. Knowledge is power so what you need is as much knowledge as you can get. The more you know, the more effective you can be as you work toward achieving the success you desire. Daydreaming can help you to more clearly envision your career direction, but if it's not coupled with action, it won't get you anywhere.

Getting from Point A to Point B

In every industry, there are proven ways to get to the highest levels of that profession. Generally, you'll need a mix of knowledge about your field of choice, business contacts, and some money. The amount and order in which you acquire these can make a huge difference to the outcomes you achieve.

So why don't we frequently hear about simple hard work, knowledge, and perseverance as being the historically tested and most effective way to achieve success? Because it's not sexy. Books and seminars about becoming successful by thinking about being successful sell well because everyone is looking for a shortcut or a magic potion for finding career happiness and wealth. These sorts of products sell well for the same reason that fad diets sell well. Everyone knows how to lose weight, but we don't do it because losing weight and keeping it off isn't necessarily an enjoyable or quick process. People want results overnight, but rarely are quick results lasting ones. Editors and TV producers know that "Eat More Vegetables and Exercise Five Times a Week" isn't a headline that's going to keep their audiences interested. Instead, they want the headline "Lose 20 Pounds in a Month Without Exercising." That kind of headline will get people's attention. Likewise, people won't be attracted by the headline "Hard Work and Dedication Lead to Success." They want to see "Think Your Way to Becoming a Millionaire."

You have to get out there in the world and make things happen for yourself.

When I look at how various types of entrepreneurs have achieved career success, a frequent pattern I see is that they had a dream about what they wanted to do but, initially, didn't know how to achieve their goals. Once they plugged into groups of people within their desired industry, they not only began to learn how to become successful within that industry, they also made valuable connections with others in and around their industry who could help them. Typically, after learning more about how to advance within their chosen industry, they would then develop and execute a plan to achieve their business goals. That is a very traditional way to become successful.

Look at it another way in the chart below. It shows some of the most common paths entrepreneurs take as they pursue career success:

have a dream	need skills	**go to university**	make a plan	enter desired industry
have a dream	need skills	**attend seminars**	make a plan	enter desired industry
have a dream	need skills	**read books**	make a plan	enter desired industry
have a dream	need skills	**get a mentor**	make a plan	enter desired industry
have a dream	need skills	**get work experience**	make a plan	enter desired industry

As you can see, the steps leading to success are pretty much the same for the most common routes listed above. The only difference is the middle step, and even that is simply a slight variation on methods used to acquire knowledge.

Business is Business in Any Business

Personally, I don't find any aspect of business magical. Despite the jargon beloved by those in the corporate world, business is pretty straightforward. Buy low, sell high. Offer great products and services at a fair price. Treat customers well. It's really that simple, just on different scales depending on the size of the business. The principles don't change, just the size of the business.

I worked in ecommerce before the dot-com crash. I remember how shocked I was to discover that business people were so mesmerized by this new selling medium that they willingly disregarded their business sense, as they fell in love with the prospect of easy money. Consequently, the dot-com crash was no surprise to me. The signs of failure were all around. Despite what some in ecommerce were saying at the time, the need to provide customers with excellent products and customer service didn't disappear simply because customers were now buying products online.

The decadent disregard of proven business practices during the dot-com boom was appalling. Recent university graduates with no practical business experience were receiving millions of dollars from venture capital firms eager to cash in on the Internet gold rush. Companies were allowing their employees to bring their pets to work; the sound of barking dogs during a conference call was considered a sign of a modern, forward-thinking company. Employees could skateboard through the office, while meetings with important clients were being conducted. Why? Heaven only knows, but it was fashionable at the time.

Even more fashionable was the crafting of bizarre job titles to provide the illusion that a company had a flat management structure. I must emphasize the word "illusion" because it was nothing more than a catchy way to make a company look modern. The simple fact was that the "Customer Service Dude" still reported to the "Customer Service Guru" who reported to the "Marketing Wizard" who then reported to the "Marketing Czar" and so on. The layers of management were still there, they just had silly job titles that confused customers and vendors alike.

I remember networking with others in ecommerce and hearing about dot-coms where the management thought a reasonable cost per customer was $75, even though the average sale was only $10. They didn't stay in business very long. Why did so many of these businesspeople ignore their training in traditional business strategies that have worked throughout history? The answer is simple: they were dazzled by the novelty of the Internet and the prospect of making millions in ecommerce. They stopped viewing business in a sensible way and began to see it as some sort of mystical process.

As I would hear ridiculous sales projections being thrown around during meetings, I would often ask, "Where do you think these dramatic sales increases will come from? If we don't have those sales figures now, what will drive all of this additional income? Is it a reasonable and practical expectation to think that consumers who have been buying these same products for decades will suddenly purchase significantly *more* of these products simply because the items can now be viewed on a computer screen instead of only in a store or a catalog? Does that make mathematical sense?" I would typically receive a you-just-don't-get-it-because-you're-so-old-school look in response.

It turns out I was right. Disregarding the traditional rules of business was a primary reason behind the massive dot-com bust in the early 2000s. Just as a disregard of proven business strategies resulted in so many dot-coms going out of business, so too will such disregard work against a creative entrepreneur striving to become successful.

Don't Be Afraid to Fail

Failure is a part of life, and, unfortunately, American society has become averse to failure to the point where people are often afraid to even try and compete. Venturing out into the exciting, and sometimes frustrating, world of entrepreneurship isn't for the faint of heart. It takes the same kind of pioneering spirit that built America and made it strong.

Don't be afraid to fail because, if your fear keeps you paralyzed in a constant state of inaction, you'll never get off the launchpad. Likewise, don't be afraid to knock on doors because the more doors you try, the more doors will open. Opportunity will rarely actively seek you.

You needn't be afraid to ask questions as you explore your chosen field and the opportunities within it. I remember a work colleague once commenting to me that I asked a lot of questions. I thought that was an odd comment because I have always figured that through questioning, we can all learn more. I frequently encounter people, particularly in the corporate world, who are afraid to ever ask a question and reveal that there is something they don't know. There is no value in that kind of attitude. I don't trust people who pretend to know everything because *no one* knows everything. I have infinitely more respect for a professional who is willing to do some research or consult with an expert on a particular subject to ensure that any business decisions made will be wise decisions based on good information.

I have failed countless times as I have worked to build my business. While, admittedly, failing is no fun, I did learn each time and then used those lessons to improve my efforts in subsequent ventures. This process of refining my methods with each effort has served to strengthen and improve my work, my expertise, and my confidence. When I share business information with a client, I can do so confidently because I have tried so many different things that I know with certainty what will work and what won't. I can guide someone else because I have already made my own mistakes, and I can help others avoid those same mistakes.

Obviously, no one wants to make huge mistakes that will permanently harm their reputation or expensive mistakes that will bankrupt them. Generally speaking, if you are judicious and reasonable in your decision making, your failures are likely to be kept to a minimum, and you'll typically learn valuable lessons from them.

Learning What You Need for Success

My goal is to teach you about critical functions you'll need to know to get up and running and start earning money as soon as possible. That doesn't mean that my book, or anyone else's for that matter, is an all-inclusive volume containing everything you'll ever need to know. It is important to never stop learning because there is a tremendous amount of information out there, and the landscape is always changing.

Remember that when you speak to professionals in your chosen industry, they will easily be able to tell if you don't know what you're talking about. I recall a casual conversation with a new acquaintance who had just gotten a position as Director of Marketing. Having just met him, I took an interest in our shared profession and casually asked him a few questions about what he did, just to make polite conversation. As a working marketer, it was immediately clear to me that he didn't understand the marketing profession at all. I later learned that he only got the position because of someone he knew in the industry.

Creating success in business requires more than just a cursory knowledge of industry terms. It is important to know how to apply business concepts in the field of your choice. Without that information, how can you effectively negotiate? How can you ensure you won't be taken advantage of by more business-savvy individuals?

Imagine finally getting the opportunity you've always dreamt of, in which you can sell your product or service on a national or international scale. You're in a boardroom with a huge marble table. The top-level decision makers from the company with which you're negotiating are all focused on your prospective profitability. You're negotiating what each party will bring to the business relationship and how revenue will be distributed. If you don't understand how business works, things could quickly spiral out of control, and you could end up being steamrollered right out of profits that should rightfully be yours. Don't allow this to happen to you. Remember, the more information you have, the greater your potential for profitable success.

If you don't have experience in business, there are a number of options available to you that can help you get up to speed. Fortunately, knowledge and information are readily available and often free or very inexpensive. Exposing yourself to as much information as possible helps you. When you're new at something, you often don't even know what questions to ask because you don't yet know what you don't know about a given field of study.

Certainly, you can attain knowledge at a university but, depending upon your chosen career path, there may be other equally effective ways. On top of that, even if you have a university degree, there may still be plenty of useful information that you were never taught while you were working to earn your degree.

Below are some effective ways to gain information that can help to provide the tools you need to advance your career and increase your profitability:

University and vocational programs

These are the kinds of programs that offer nationally and, sometimes, internationally recognized degrees. An increasing number of these are available online, which can help new entrepreneurs who are still working a day job to pay the bills. High costs are often a challenging factor.

Business seminars and instructional programs

These can range from hundreds of dollars to tens of thousands. Really good programs on the higher end of the price spectrum can offer a distillation of the most important marketing concepts that entrepreneurs need to build successful businesses. Some of these programs focus on particular entrepreneurial niches by offering programs designed specifically for groups such as authors, speakers, or investors. To make sure you're choosing the best program for you, investigate programs thoroughly and try to speak with people who have taken them to get a better idea of whether a certain program is right for you. Don't be afraid to ask questions because any reputable company will be happy to answer them.

Some companies that offer these programs also sell lower-priced DVDs containing some of the information covered in the seminars. While attending the seminars definitely offers a fuller and more enriching experience, in which you can network with other professionals and even ask questions that pertain to your specific career goals, pre-packaged DVDs can still offer tremendous value and education. As with live seminars and programs, just investigate before you buy.

Local non-credit, enrichment courses

A very affordable way to learn from local experts is to attend non-credit adult education classes. I have taught these kinds of courses at local learning centers and high schools for many years, and people frequently tell me they find this type of learning to be less stressful than classes in which a grade is received. It can be a fun and more affordable way to learn what you'll need for your business, while networking with other professionals in your community.

Books

I love books, I really do. They provide a great way to learn a tremendous amount of information that can also be kept for reference purposes. I write in many of my books and highlight the parts that I find most valuable so I can easily find those passages again in the future.

Another option is ebooks, which are available in a variety of formats to be read on different types of mobile devices. These are generally less expensive than printed books.

If you don't want to buy books, you can always go to the library. If you have trouble finding what you're looking for, be sure to ask your librarian. Many libraries share books so your selection can likely be ordered.

Also, if you don't have time to read much because you spend a lot of time traveling, an increasing number of books are available in an audio format so you can learn while you travel.

Experts on the Internet

We live in a wonderful age in which information is more readily available than ever before. By simply getting online, you can instantly have access to loads of free information from industry experts who share their advice with you on their websites and through their email newsletters. (I'm actually one of them, and you can sign up for my free email newsletter on the home page of my website: www.raiaking.net. I'm happy to share marketing tips that can help you build your business and make more money!) Many of these experts even offer free or low-cost teleseminars and webinars that can provide you with valuable business advice.

In addition to information on websites from experts in your field, you can read articles by journalists who specialize in interviewing all sorts of industry professionals about various business topics that can provide you with valuable information. These interviews can easily be found by typing keywords that pertain to your topic of interest into a search engine. Try rephrasing your keywords to get a variety of results. This may take a bit more time than attending a business seminar, but you can't beat the price.

CHAPTER 2

Creative People in a Non-Creative World

Being Creative

Creative people know they're different. As a creative person, you learn that your mind is operating on a different level from non-creative people. Certainly there are multitudinous tests you can take and books that address the differences between creative and non-creative types, but they only confirm what you already knew. They don't necessarily tell you what to do about it from a business standpoint.

As a creative person myself, I understand what you're going through. Like you, I have felt the frustration of seeing potential where others see only a lack of opportunity. Creative people who have vision and drive are rarely the kinds of people who can find happiness by following other people's rules and other people's schedules. To a creative person, being trapped in a cycle of waking up, going to a mundane corporate job, bringing more office work home, going to sleep, and then waking up only to start the same cycle all over again is tantamount to a nightmare.

Many creative people feel trapped in jobs that make them miserable because no one around them shares their vision of the world. This is why so many successful creative types break out on their own to forge their own future. Is it scary? Certainly, but it *can* be done. The key is doing it wisely without putting your financial security in jeopardy.

When you have a clear vision of how to create prosperity and a better life for yourself, it is stifling to have to deny yourself the chance to achieve your desires because you don't have the time or resources to fulfill them. You find that your daily work, which you're doing primarily to pay the bills, is getting in the way of the real work that you passionately want to do because it's your true calling.

It's okay to dream, as long as you couple those dreams with action.

Many in the corporate world don't take creative people seriously because they view creative types as dreamers. It's okay to dream, as long as you couple those dreams with action. Simply dreaming without actively taking steps to make those dreams come true is useless and won't get you any closer to your goals.

You've probably been thinking about your dream career for a long time. You may have even written up plans for attaining the success you desire. As you go through this book, you will see examples of exercises that will help you to create a strong personal plan for achieving your career goals. Remember that there is no reason you shouldn't be able to create the type of life you want; you deserve career success and happiness just as much as anyone else. You *can* do it!

Getting Started

I have been teaching the information in this book for about 15 years, and in that time I have often asked people what has been holding them back from achieving their career dreams. The most common answers I receive are that people have a lack of time and a lack of money. People also frequently tell me that they have a general idea of what they want to do or some vague notion of the direction in which they want to head, but they don't know how to get started.

I will address these issues throughout the book. I should tell you up front that my philosophy on career development is shaped by my views on the following three components:

Money

I view money as a means to an end, not solely as an end in itself. Essentially, money equals freedom. Money is like the game pieces with which we can more successfully play the game; it merely gives us more options in life. Greed, however, is useless and harmful not only to the person it afflicts but to those around that person. Greed can ruin relationships, businesses, and lives. My approach to acquiring money is to be able to use it as a tool in life, but not to let it run your life. Throughout this book I advise people to be judicious with funds, not careless. Taking your focus off of achieving your desired career and placing it solely on the acquisition of money will usually get you off track and slow your progress toward career success, rather than expedite it.

Time

In my view, this is the most important resource we have and is infinitely more valuable than any amount of money. When comparing money with time, time is more scarce because it is spent at a consistent rate whether you use it wisely or not. You can't save it to use later, and you can't get more by earning interest on it. If you ever had any doubt about the worth of money compared to the worth of time, imagine being on a sinking ship and being offered your choice of either a billion dollars or a cheap, plastic raft to get you back to land and into the arms of those you love. Suddenly, the money is worthless.

Realistic Goals

While you can certainly achieve your career dreams, it is important to realize that none of us can ignore the realities of life. For example, if someone in their forties always wanted to be a teen model, it would be a bit too late for that . . . just a bit. However, this person could still get into other types of modeling. It's a big world out there so keep your eyes, heart, and mind open to possibilities you may not have known existed. One obstacle doesn't necessarily mean you need to abandon your dreams completely, they may simply need slight modification. The good news is that you may actually discover wonderful surprises in the process that never occurred to you before.

Dealing With Anger and Frustration

Conventional wisdom dictates that we must cheerfully accept all career adversity with grace and simply endure a plethora of platitudes such as, "Keep your chin up," and "Life's not fair." The problem is that when life gives us lemons, we hardly feel like making lemonade. Does this make us horrible people? Of course not . . . it just means we're human.

So often, I have heard people, particularly corporate types, say, "You aren't identified by your occupation. It's just a job."

Perhaps that is the case for some people, but when your desired career is an integral part of your personality and a true passion, it is far more than just a job. For creative people in particular, what we do with our lives identifies us. Job titles carry with them a tremendous number of connotations: painter, lawyer, musician, CEO, physician, social worker, actor, etc. Rightly or wrongly, people treat you differently depending upon your occupation and that, in turn, can have a significant effect on how you feel about yourself. Additionally, when a job is a passion instead of merely a way to earn money to pay the bills, the entire dynamic of how a person relates to his or her work is changed.

It isn't uncommon for creative people to express anger and frustration as they work to build their artistic careers. Often, such feelings are viewed as negative and counterproductive. Many experts ignore the very real experience of anger and frustration that many people, especially creative people, feel. To do so, however, is to deny an individual's humanity. We are not robots, and artists in particular are more in touch with their emotions and see things differently than non-creative types. If you're feeling angry and frustrated, you're *normal.* It only becomes a problem and an obstacle if you focus on those feelings to the exclusion of all others and allow anger to consume you and become counterproductive. Being aware that you may feel this way from time to time helps to defuse the power of the emotions and helps you to deal with your feelings more objectively. Instead of beating yourself up, feeling ashamed, or being consumed with frustration, harness that energy and use it as fuel to drive yourself toward success.

Often times, creative people in a traditional corporate setting become frustrated because they can see creative and more effective solutions to problems at work, but management won't listen to them. Corporate types feel threatened by this kind of anger because they don't understand it. Frequently, anger is nothing more than fear or frustration in disguise. What management fails to recognize is that, generally, the person who exhibits anger and frustration about the state of affairs at work is doing so because they *care* about the business running successfully. That's a *good* thing! Managers should really be far more wary of those who apathetically show up to punch a clock and couldn't care less whether the company succeeds or fails. Unfortunately, these very worker bees are frequently the ones who effortlessly sail up the corporate ladder, hence the perpetual dissatisfaction of the creative worker who is able to develop creative solutions.

When making business decisions, let logic rule over emotion.

Years ago, a psychologist who did marriage counseling told me that she could tell which marriages had a chance and which didn't as soon as a couple walked into her office. Interestingly, she said that the couples who came in angry were more likely to succeed. They were arguing because they still cared. The couples who were apathetic and said very little had already given up and stood little chance of reconciliation. The workplace is very similar.

If your employer doesn't recognize your passion for success, you may as well make it work for you in some other aspect of your life. By channeling your frustration and not allowing it to conquer you, you can use it to drive your success. When making business decisions, be sure to let logic rule over emotion because you'll make better decisions.

For those of you who are ready to give up and feel that your dreams have been crushed or that you have been sentenced to live in the mire of conformity, please take comfort in knowing that you are not the only one who feels that way. There are *millions* of others out there who feel *exactly the same way* you do. I used to feel that way. No matter how flamboyant or eccentric your self-expression, *you . . . are . . . not . . . alone.* Find strength in the knowledge that everyone has to start out somewhere and that you are continuing in a long tradition of creative entrepreneurs who have brought more warmth, texture, joy, comfort, and beauty into the world.

Finding Other Creative People

If you don't currently know other people like yourself, seek them out in your community and the surrounding areas. The Internet provides a great way to find all manner of artistic organizations for fields ranging from art and music to dance and writing.

Through community events, you can meet other people in your field and begin to make a name for yourself in your chosen profession. If you're a painter, get your paintings into art shows. If you're a musician, start playing live shows to build your professional reputation. Getting out in the community and promoting your work is the best way to promote yourself, not only to the public but also to others in your field with whom you can network to find and create new opportunities.

Certainly, in this Internet age, much can be done from home, but there is no substitute for being physically in front of people, showing them what you can do, meeting people at industry events, talking to them personally, displaying your work, etc.

Building business relationships in person will help people remember you and what you do. As they repeatedly see you working within your industry, they will become more familiar with you and be more likely to recommend your talents, products, and services to others.

CHAPTER 3

Navigating Through the Status Quo

Educational Traditions

There are a number of obstacles that keep many of us from fulfilling our true potential, not the least of which is the status quo. It seems as if all systems of education and employment are stacked against us from the very beginning. Consider your education, for a start. Whether you went to public school or private school, do you recall having any classes on entrepreneurship? I didn't think so. Class time was spent teaching traditional subjects, and often in ways that didn't even accomplish those goals effectively.

Why on earth would a math problem be presented by asking alienating questions such as, "If John has four oranges and Susan has five apples, what is the distance from New York to Chicago?" Huh??? Why not frame mathematical questions in realistic and relatable ways? Wouldn't it make sense to use these learning opportunities to teach students about amortization schedules and the workings of the stock market in age-appropriate ways that kids could understand?

Throughout school, I was convinced that I was useless at math, primarily because of the alienating manner in which it was taught. After school, I discovered, to my surprise, that as soon as dollar signs were placed in front of the numbers, I was a mathematical wizard. What changed? The application of the equations. When the math problems were relatable and presented in a real-world application, they suddenly made perfect sense.

As early as elementary school, I was keenly aware of some sort of fraud being perpetrated upon my classmates and me. When, during a spelling quiz, a student in my third grade class would ask the teacher why these spelling quizzes were so important, the teacher would inform us that we'd need to know these things for the tests in the next grade. Once in fourth grade, our next teacher would give the same response to the exact same question. The story was also the same in fifth grade, and I became suspicious of this pattern. Was there no better reason than for the sake of the tests in the next grade that we were required to learn this subject matter? In retrospect, I find it appalling that not one teacher at that early stage presented the notion to us that we could be empowered by knowledge and harness that power to create the kinds of lives we dreamed of. Not one. That is nothing short of disgraceful.

Throughout school, my classmates and I were often required to consult with individuals referred to as *guidance counselors*. These folks informed us that they would help us decide what career path to take. The discussions were typically along the lines of:

"So, what do you like to do?"

"I like to take pictures."

"Well then, you should get a job as a photographer."

How very illuminating. Thanks for the insight and sage advice.

These fine individuals neglected to mention the myriad of creative job opportunities out there. You can only imagine my surprise when I discovered that someone could have a financially successful career as a pyrotechnician, a milliner, or a chocolatier. Why were these career options never presented? All of my teachers and guidance counselors were single-mindedly focused on all students going to college or technical school, then going to work for other people. There was no instruction on forging your own way in life to become an entrepreneur. For a time commitment of twelve years of a student's life, this is a significant and unforgivable omission.

Please understand, I'm not looking to slam all teachers because I've also had some excellent teachers. The main problem, as I saw more fully when I was in the secondary education program at university, is with the education system. I saw this for myself when teachers showed me the restrictions on what they could accomplish in the classroom. Anonymous bureaucrats design a system that impedes learning instead of encouraging it, so teachers are stuck in a bad system that isn't designed to meet the needs of today's students.

The next step after high school was presumed to be university. While I was repeatedly told that this next step was the only way to true success, I remained unconvinced. The problem was that I didn't have any other good ideas because I'd just spent the previous twelve years learning absolutely nothing about entrepreneurship.

My declaration that going to a university was not the only way to earn a living was not received enthusiastically by my parents. After trying for over a year after high school to get a decent job, I learned the hard way that it was next to impossible to even get an interview for a decent job without that sacrosanct piece of paper known as a university diploma. I found that notion foolish for the simple reason that I knew plenty of knuckleheads who had essentially boozed their way through university and learned precious little as a result. Now, I was going to have to compete with these folks for jobs, and they'd win simply because of a piece of paper? Wonderful.

Reluctantly giving in, I attended university and got a bachelor of arts in English and a certificate in studio art. Suddenly, as if by magic, I was able to get job interviews.

Despite this process having worked in enabling me to get employment, to this day I remain unconvinced about it working on its own merit rather than simply because of cultural conventions. Did I learn valuable things at university? Sure I did, but I was also constantly aware of how much time was being wasted in a procedure that seemed more like a self-sustaining business practice than anything else. The entire process was much like the traditional record industry practice of releasing every album in relatively the same format of ten to fifteen songs. I likened the courses that pertained directly to my field of pursuit to the hit songs. The rest of the courses, taken in the name of becoming well rounded, were like filler songs used to populate the rest of the slots on the album simply because "that's just how it's done."

Additionally sad was a history professor's comment that reminded me of the comments from my elementary school teachers about why we needed to take spelling quizzes. I'll never forget it, a student in my history class asked why we needed to know about the historical events we were studying, and the professor replied that we needed to know so that when we went to cocktail parties, we'd be able to have intelligent discussions with other people. *Are you kidding me?????* This woman, who had been teaching her entire life and was now in her fifties, had no better answer than that? She had never paused for consideration about the value of her profession? Never?

Having since returned to university to earn an MBA, I still have very mixed feelings about the entire process. While there is certainly value in a formal education because you can gain experience that is more difficult to get as an autodidact, such as being challenged by experts in their respective fields so you can get feedback and refine your skills, there is still a tremendous amount of waste and inefficiency in the standardized formal education process.

Going to university does offer some shortcuts to learning that being self taught may not accomplish, for example, you needn't reinvent the wheel because all of the mistakes that other innovators made along the way are presented to you so you can learn quickly. At the same time, being encumbered by so many *filler classes*, as I call them, slows your progress toward achieving success. If an associate's degree was as valued in the workplace as a bachelor's degree, everyone would simply get an associate's degree. For some inexplicable reason, however, employers and society in general seem to find those additional gym classes and throwaway electives worthy of a significant increase in annual salary and significant prestige.

Lessons From the Corporate World

Upon entering the corporate world I made the alarming discovery that, despite what I'd been told in school, most companies are not meritocracies and that it really is not *what* but *who* you know. I encountered the world of Human Resources professionals who serve as the gatekeepers between employees and employers. It appears that their primary focus is not looking for talent but determining ways to weed people out of the running for positions. In my many interactions with HR people, I typically encountered an almost robotic search for keywords with seemingly little concern for anything else. Yet another process that simply doesn't make sense, thus delivering mediocre results.

My dream had always been to work in music professionally, but I was constantly told that I couldn't make it in music because it was all about who you know. You can imagine how angry I was to discover that the same was true in the corporate world. It made me wish I'd pursued music, after all. At least I actually knew some people in that industry. In the corporate world, I didn't know anybody, and it hurt me from day one.

Like so many creative entrepreneurs before you, you have most likely seen that your dreams, ambitions, and passions will be squelched, if not completely extinguished, by the traditional corporate world. It is not constructed for creative people and, as a creative person, you have drives that non-creative people don't understand or appreciate. You can offer qualities that an HR manager won't be able to detect by using mindless keyword searches. Many in corporate life consider creative people to be useless dreamers who don't want to work hard but, with this view, they fail to recognize the power of innovation and how it can literally translate into huge profits.

CHAPTER 4

Do You Love the Job or Just the Title?

Recognizing Your True Passion

Considering the manner in which most corporations view creative people, it can be quite challenging for such individuals to make a decent living using their talents within a traditional corporate framework. If you have chosen a non-traditional creative career path, it is important to realistically recognize your creative talents and embrace them. It is equally critical to recognize your weaknesses, to ensure that they don't undermine your success as you work to build your career.

It is wise to take some time and give very serious thought to what you really want to do. Being vague can unnecessarily waste valuable time and resources. Think about your competition in the field you've chosen. Knowing how your talents stack up against your competitors' talents is just as important in creative fields as in non-creative fields. Being realistic about your abilities is crucial.

I have taught writing classes for many years and frequently come across people who will eagerly tell me about the novel they've been writing for the last ten years. They enjoy the reaction of classmates who are impressed by their apparent dedication and drive. They'll tell me that they've always wanted to write professionally yet, interestingly, these are often the very individuals who never got so much as a magazine article published because, in truth, they're just not really that passionate about writing. So why do they profess a love of writing?

Because they like the *idea* of being a writer but not the actual process required to become one. At the end of the day, they really just like the job title, but not the actual job.

Not to only point the finger at others, I admittedly had experience with my own creative misdirection, in the realm of music. At the age of 14, I decided that I wanted to write songs so I learned to play guitar. I played well enough to write very basic songs, but by no means did I play well. I would practice but quickly became bored. I wanted to want to, if you know what I mean. I sang in all sorts of bands from pop to heavy metal to folk, and the entire time I kept trying to become proficient at playing an instrument because I didn't want to just be a singer. When I realized that I wasn't cut out to be a lead guitarist (and not much of a rhythm guitarist for that matter), I tried bass guitar, which was an even bigger disaster. Next, I tried drums, which I actually enjoyed far more than guitar but, unfortunately, I was more interested in my drum teacher than my drums.

Interestingly, the entire time I was trying to find a passion for an instrument, I was writing constantly and taking it for granted. I would stop playing guitar to write lyrics for music I hadn't even written yet. I'd happily and easily write lyrics for music that my musician friends wanted lyrics for but couldn't write. I'd put aside homework to write articles just for fun. I'd write humorous pieces for no reason other than to amuse myself. I'd stay up until one in the morning to write . . . *anything*, as long as I was writing.

Looking back, I can't believe I didn't recognize it sooner. I was in love with the idea of being a songwriter, but my true passion was writing words, not necessarily music. I love music passionately yet, sadly, creating it wasn't my strength.

It eventually began to dawn on me when I looked at friends who were brilliant instrumentalists. I saw that they were so passionate about playing that they'd neglect other responsibilities in order to play. They'd choose practicing over hanging out with friends. Their parents would scream at them over bad grades in school, and they'd hardly look up from their instruments. It seemed as if they'd continue playing even if it were illegal, simply because they were so passionate that they *couldn't* stop. They spent every spare moment playing just like I spent every spare minute writing . . . .

At last, the penny dropped.

What artistic pursuit consumes nearly every waking moment?

It's perfectly natural to be passionate about something yet not have the drive or ability to create the very thing about which you're passionate. There's also no shame in recognizing that reality. I love beautiful gardens, yet I'm no good with plants. I enjoy fine cuisine yet, when I'm cooking, I'd be wise to wear safety goggles and surround the kitchen with caution tape. Recognizing where your real talents lie only strengthens you and enables you to gain professional ground more quickly.

What are you so passionate about that you'd rather be doing that activity than doing anything else? What artistic pursuit consumes nearly every waking moment? Increase your awareness about what truly motivates you, and let that help guide you to your true calling.

Motivation and Competition

Every profession has its own structure and accepted ways of reaching successively higher levels of achievement within that profession. It is important to recognize the obstacle course that lies before you so that you can effectively navigate through it. Don't let one or two bad experiences stop your progression forward. Instead, learn from those experiences, continually strive for professional excellence, and keep working.

It is important to recognize the impetus for your drive toward a successful creative career. What are you in it for? Your love of the art? Fame? Money? Ego? While these factors can coexist, they are still separate components. Knowing why you are seeking to achieve your goals can help you make decisions about what direction you should take, when faced with various opportunities. For example, if money is your primary driving force, there may be areas in which you're willing to compromise that someone primarily concerned with building a career around a love for art may not be willing to compromise. There's nothing at all wrong with that, but having an awareness of what truly drives you will help in your decision making.

If you want to have a career in an artistic field, you need to earn money. This changes the way you approach decisions and introduces an urgency that a simple hobby lacks.

A major source of frustration for aspiring artists is in trying to manage their image. An example of this is the exasperation an actor feels when casting directors don't see what he's really capable of in an audition. He only has a few minutes to convey his abilities and secure the job. It is frustrating when you feel that you are not seen in the way you want to be seen. It can be difficult for artists to view themselves as a "product" to be sold yet, once you enter the realm of an artistic *business*, you need to sell your image and talent just like you'd sell any other product.

Thinking in those terms, consider that people only see a glimpse of your abilities when they see you perform, hear one of your songs, see one of your photographs, or are exposed to the finished products of your creative skills in some other form. Because of that, it is important to try to influence their perception as much as possible. Think of every contact with the public as a TV commercial that advertises what you do. People quickly form impressions and attitudes about products based solely on ads. That means you have approximately 30 seconds to set a favorable impression. There is so much competing for people's attention that you're lucky to get a cursory glance, let alone undivided attention. This makes it even more important to differentiate yourself from your competition.

Realistically Appraising Your Talent

Another important component in pursuing a career in a creative field is being realistic. By their very nature, many creative endeavors can be more difficult to judge because they are more art than science. It's simple to identify a successful retail sales campaign in the corporate world because the sales numbers can easily be measured. It is more difficult, however, to measure the talent of a painter because the artistic value of the painting is open to interpretation. A useful way to gauge your talent is to get out there amongst your fellow artists. Challenge yourself and present your talents to the community of professionals in your chosen field. Welcome constructive criticism with an open mind. Sure, it can be difficult to hear a critique of your efforts, when you have poured your heart and soul into them, but it can give you valuable insight into how others view your work.

No one wants to be like the clueless singer on a nationally televised talent show who declares confidently that everyone tells her how great her voice is just before she gets blasted by the judges for being a poor performer. Over and over, we see these kinds of singers looking genuinely shocked when the judges tell them that they can't sing well. Why? Because they've never before gotten opinions from industry professionals.

Get feedback from working professionals in your chosen industry.

To ensure that this doesn't happen to you, take steps that will help you gain a realistic perspective of what you have to offer and how it will be perceived by prospective customers. Instead of solely surrounding yourself with well-meaning people who only tell you positive things, get feedback from working professionals in your chosen industry. People who work in your field will have the experience to know what industry decision-makers are looking for when they hire artists or what the public are looking for when they buy products from artists. That's not to say that professionals can never be wrong, but their feedback will likely give you a considerably more accurate view of the marketplace value of your talent.

Keep in mind, when you get feedback, you certainly don't want to change everything you do based on the input from only one person. If you do that, you'll be changing your course of action so frequently that you'll be unable to move forward. It is wiser to seek out several opinions from professionals, customers, and prospects and look for trends. If you hear similar comments about the same issue repeatedly, then it is something you should consider changing or modifying. By looking for trends, you'll be able to address the salient points that come up, and you can dramatically improve your performance, thereby increasing your chances of success. This is true for any kind of creative endeavor, not just performing.

Going back to the example of singers trying to win televised talent competitions, how can these folks improve their chances of success? Clearly, professing a dedication to their art is insufficient. What is needed is to take action by immersing themselves in the *business* of singing. This will build confidence and skill that is only attained through experience. Training with a professional voice coach will provide expertise and finesse that can help a vocalist perfect their strongest skills, while strengthening their weaknesses. Trying to get work as a singer will help a vocalist see the marketability of his or her talent. All kinds of informal, yet valuable, lessons will be learned by going through these experiences. Simply singing in isolation at home will deny a vocalist this type of valuable knowledge, hence there will be a huge potential for unawareness of how marketable the individual's talent is. That kind of unawareness can undermine even the most well executed business efforts.

Will This Really Make You Happy?

When trying to determine which creative career path is for you, there are many considerations. Think about your goals and tolerances. Traveling the world doing live theater may sound glamorous but, if you value spending time with your family, it may end up making you unhappy in the end because you'd have to sacrifice a tremendous amount of time that could otherwise be spent with your family. That doesn't mean you can't work in the theater, but you may be happier in an occupation within that field that doesn't have you out on the road for most of the year.

As you're evaluating your next moves in working toward achieving your desired career, it is important to thoroughly think through all of your personal priorities before you begin planning. It is critical to be focused and use time wisely so being absolutely certain about what will bring you happiness in life is essential.

A major issue that I frequently encounter in workshops I teach is that many people are inadvertently setting themselves up for disaster. They have good intentions and are developing ideas about the career they see themselves in but often, when we discuss the day-to-day realities of such a career, we discover that the career they've been aiming for may not actually be the best choice to bring them the happiness they desire.

Take some time to seriously consider what you really value in life, as you determine your career path in a creative field. Decisions you make now can affect you dramatically years from now so set aside a couple of hours without distraction to spend some time in thoughtful contemplation.

When you take time to concentrate on your personal priorities, think about how you would prioritize considerations of life, such as finances, material wealth, spirituality, leadership, privacy, fame, security, stability, career longevity, excitement, friendship, and family relationships. There may even be other considerations I haven't mentioned here that are very important to you.

I find it helpful to write down the various priorities being considered and listing pros and cons under each one. By keeping track of these issues on paper, it becomes easier to see where there could be potential conflict, before you have invested a tremendous amount of time, energy, and money on endeavors that may not actually be a good fit for your desires. As you go through the exercise of deciding where your priorities are concentrated, remember that there are no right or wrong answers. What is right for *you* is right. Everyone's determinations for themselves will be different, and that's okay.

I remember a number of years ago, I took myself through this exercise when I was considering becoming a certified gemologist so I could become a buyer for a major jewelry manufacturer. I even got so far as to request the application from the Gemological Institute of America. I was that serious. Just before filling it out, I sat down and thought about my personal priorities compared with the job opportunities that awaited me if I became a gemologist. I realized that, as a buyer, I'd most likely be on the road frequently, which was exactly what I didn't want. I wanted a career in which I could spend more time at home, not less. In the end, I realized that taking that path wouldn't fit well into my priorities. Fortunately, I realized this before committing huge amounts of time and money toward getting certified.

A good example of recognizing life priorities is one from an interview I read a number of years ago. In the interview, an English journalist said that she had initially considered going into acting as she began her career. Interestingly, she said that the reason she didn't become an actor was because credibility was very important to her, and she felt that she wouldn't have the same credibility as an actor that she would as a news journalist. Recognizing her priorities early on, she took the course of action that was right for her.

If someone places a high value on privacy, working in the entertainment industry as a performer could compromise privacy. However, there are certainly plenty of opportunities behind the scenes that are just as creative and satisfying that enable a creative professional to maintain his or her privacy. Again, it all comes down to personal preferences.

There are all sorts of creative jobs in the world that offer just the right balance for people with different priorities and tolerances. Spending the time considering what is the best fit for you can not only make sure you are working toward a career that will satisfy your soul but also save a tremendous amount of time and money by helping you to avoid time-consuming and expensive mistakes along the way.

Additionally, there is a huge difference between running *to* something and running *from* something. While both of these actions may take you to the same place, the reasons and the means by which you arrive are completely different. Making sure that your targeted career is more than merely a job that seems better than what you have now really does matter.

Birds of a Feather

Another lesson I have learned is that surrounding yourself with other driven people will, in turn, help you advance your own business. Like it or not, we are all heavily influenced by the company that we keep. It is common to see very successful people surrounded by other successful people. They may not have all started out being successful, but they eventually attained success. Likewise, it isn't unusual to see unsuccessful people, who may actually have brilliant ideas, toiling away in obscurity, never to achieve success.

Early in my career, I wasted a lot of time because I didn't have the tools I needed to maximize my productivity. Additionally, I spent far too much time surrounded by people who had no direction in life. In such situations, it's easy to get dragged down and influenced by a contagious defeatist attitude. While valuable weeks, months, and years of your life are ticking away, time can easily be wasted trying to reinvent the wheel, instead of learning efficiency from other people's mistakes and achievements.

Does this mean you should abandon your friends and only spend time with successful people? Of course not, but if you don't already spend at least some time with people focused on success, it would be wise to begin meeting some new people to add to your roster of friends.

There is much learning to be gained from universities and books, but there are also many informal lessons that can be learned from others who are traveling on the path to business success. By spending quality time with these people and circulating in their circles, you will learn lessons you'd never learn in school. As trends evolve within your industry, not to mention along with technology and social media, you will be well positioned to acquire the hottest information on the street so you can begin implementing it within your own business immediately. The more quickly you can acquire critical knowledge and apply it, the more quickly you can become successful in your chosen field.

CHAPTER 5

Staying Motivated

Dealing With Distractions

While you're working to build your career, it is likely that you will have a multitude of other demanding things going on in your life at the same time. You may be working a full-time job just to pay the bills, until you can do what you really want to do for a living. You may be getting married, having children, taking classes, getting divorced, or any number of other things. Even though you may be enthusiastic about trying to achieve the success you've always dreamt of, there will be times when you'll feel very tired and run down. It can be easy to slip into depression or lethargy when you're putting forth such a great deal of effort and not seeing results as quickly as you'd like.

Balance is critical to stay in the race for the long-term.

Don't beat yourself up over these feelings because they're perfectly normal. We all have complex feelings and expectations, and we can't run endlessly without getting tired or frustrated when it seems as though nothing is going according to plan, despite our hard work. Remember that most successful people have failed repeatedly as they work toward success. That's a big part of the reason why they eventually achieve success, because they don't give up. They learn from their experiences, both good and bad, and use that to fuel the fire of their career passion to get them to the next level.

Physical Challenges

While being driven toward a goal is certainly a good thing, it's important to remember that you also need to take care of yourself. Sometimes, you'll need to take a bit of a break to clear your mind and recharge your batteries. Those breaks aren't a waste of time, but rather an opportunity to take in new energy and influences that you can use to renew your dedication and strengthen your efforts. Just think of how you might feel if you only got three or four hours of sleep every night for a week. By the end of the week you'd feel pretty lousy and wouldn't be as creative and productive as you are when you're well-rested and feeling energized. By taking care of yourself, rather than driving yourself into the ground by working too much, you'll find that you can produce a higher quality of work in less time. This kind of efficiency can propel you toward success even faster.

I have seen too many people try to work endless hours by sustaining themselves on little more than coffee and cigarettes, thinking that this would get them across the finish line more quickly. Instead, I saw them become burned-out and unproductive. Likewise, mass quantities of sugar and caffeine aren't the answer either. Just like an athlete preparing for an important competition, you want to maintain a healthy diet, in addition to getting proper rest and exercise. Balance is critical to stay in the race for the long-term.

Emotional Challenges

So much of what will test you will not be physical but emotional. Well-meaning friends and family will tell you not take rejection personally, but it's difficult when you're so passionate about what you want to do with your life. In many ways, it identifies you and, as such, is almost an extension of you. It's a completely different mind-set from a job in which you would simply punch a time card. People who don't have that passion within themselves may find such a concept difficult to understand because they've never felt that way before.

While you may often hear people tell you that you're just dreaming and you'll never achieve anything, it is important to have someone in your life to provide much needed emotional support, especially during times when your confidence is waning. That's not to say, however, that you should ignore constructive criticism that could actually be beneficial to you. For example, if someone wants to pursue a career as a singer and is patently tone deaf, ignoring the advice of loved ones who are simply trying to spare the prospective vocalist from embarrassment and wasted time would be unwise. If, on the other hand, you are qualified to pursue your desired career, you may find that a common reason people tell you it's impossible is simply because they've never personally known anyone who has been successful in that field.

Having a friend with whom you can share your little victories and losses can go a long way when you're starting to waver over career decisions. It's even better if your support person is already a professional in your chosen field because this individual can be realistic about whether you can actually find success in exactly the form you envision. Sometimes, you may find that some modification to your career plan is needed, but that's okay. It's all part of the refinement process that will get you to where you want to be.

You will undoubtedly feel overwhelmed at times, but trying to be proactive before frustration sets in can revive your endurance. When I feel that way, I recall my years of singing lessons, in which various vocal coaches would explain how to hit high notes reliably and with strength. As a mezzo-soprano, I frequently found myself having to sing very high vocal parts that would be more comfortable for a soprano. One particular vocal coach used to say that, instead of sliding up to hit a high note, I should come down on top of it. I wondered, "How the heck can I come down on top of the note, if I can't even reach it in the first place?" After some work, however, I understood what she meant and learned the technique that enabled me to do the very thing I thought I was incapable of doing.

Likewise, as you work, try to get on top of things, instead of letting things get on top of you. It may sound like an inconsequential distinction, but it can make all the difference in the world. Suddenly, instead of struggling to reach up toward the seemingly unreachable, you'll find yourself being able to work more comfortably and with better control.

CHAPTER 6

Image Management

Presenting a Professional Business Image

It has never been easier for entrepreneurs to present themselves and their fledgling businesses in a professional manner. New technology has brought us companies that allow people to purchase small runs of attractive business stationery at affordable prices. Websites can be made for free or for a very low price and professional email campaigns can be created and managed for a small monthly fee. Now, more than ever, solo entrepreneurs can effectively build a customer base and maintain contact with customers, while projecting a professional image from day one.

It makes sense to create the most professional image you can reasonably afford. Certainly, you need to be judicious with money, since you don't want to bankrupt your business, but you also don't want to project an image that makes you appear to be an amateur. Prospects pick up on every element of your presentation, whether consciously or subconsciously, and it affects their purchasing decisions, including from which business they will buy and how much they'll spend. Projecting a professional image gives customers confidence in your ability to deliver what they expect. Obviously, those expectations need to be met to ensure continued business and referrals.

Interacting With Prospects and Customers

In addition to visual materials, such as marketing pieces and websites, it is also critical to project a professional image in regard to how you interact with prospects and customers. A prime example is dealing with people over the phone. When a potential customer is interested enough to take the time to pick up the phone and call your business, you have an excellent chance of making a sale. To maximize the opportunity of closing more sales, make sure that anyone who answers your business phone is very professional and eager to help callers. When you're unavailable, make sure that your voice mail message sounds professional, and be sure to return calls within a reasonable amount of time.

I think it's wise to have a business line that is separate from your home phone number. You probably don't want your home phone number on your website and your marketing materials, anyway, and it's nice to have a buffer between work life and home life. When you work from a home office, the lines between home and work can easily become blurred so a separate line can help you maintain some distance from work, when you need to take a break for the sake of your sanity. Additionally, you can then relax when answering your home phone because you know you don't have to answer with a business greeting when picking up calls from unfamiliar phone numbers.

Social Media Accounts

When creating social media accounts for your business, be sure to keep these separate from your personal social media accounts. This can make it less likely that a friend will post personal information or pictures on your business site for all of your customers to see. It can be okay to share a bit of your personal life with your clients, but you probably don't want a lengthy conversation about a graduation picnic you attended this past weekend going back and forth on the page intended for your business. It looks unprofessional and distracts people from the reason you created your business page in the first place . . . to do business!

Working From Home

Since it is helpful to keep home life and work separate, it is also valuable to have a designated work area that you use specifically for business. You don't necessarily have to set up an entire room in your home as an office, but having a clear desk space, a business phone, and a storage area strictly designated only for your work-related paperwork and materials can help you stay organized and focused. The storage area is particularly important because you want to have business materials readily available just when you need them.

I have known many people who like to get away from their home office to work. Many of them go to a local coffeehouse and some go to coworking spaces, which are growing increasingly popular among entrepreneurs. Personally, I prefer to work in my home office because I can avoid the distractions of a public space, but there is no right or wrong. The good news is that what's right for you is right.

CHAPTER 7

The Issue of Age in Entertainment

Hazards of Starting Young in the Entertainment Industry

Age is an interesting subject. It can work to your advantage or, conversely, it can work against you. In American culture, it is clear that advertisers, Hollywood, and the media are all obsessed with age. To watch American television today, one would think that no one over 40 (or at least no one who *looks* older than 40) even exists. It's reminiscent of the 1976 science fiction film *Logan's Run*, in which no one was allowed to live beyond the age of 30.

Interestingly, while youth is worshipped, particularly in Hollywood, it can actually be a tremendous occupational hazard in the very same business that values it so greatly. In the entertainment industry, you have to be young, but not *too* young. We have seen multitudinous child stars who have been used up and thrown away by the profit-hungry Hollywood machine. We have also witnessed the wreckage of former teen idols strewn across our pop-cultural landscape. Why? Because whatever age you are when people get to know you, in their minds, you will be that age forever. Since being on television introduces you to vast numbers of people all at once, being a child star can cause you to be perennially viewed as a child in the minds of the public.

We have all seen talented artists struggle with trying to reinvent their images. Consider singer, songwriter, and producer Deborah Gibson. As a teenager in the eighties, she was signed to a major record label and quickly became a regular on MTV.

Singles from her debut album topped the music charts, as she broke all sorts of industry achievement records. After being so successful as a legitimate artist and producer, her image as a young teen star became difficult to shake, as she matured, because many in the public were reluctant to view Gibson as an adult.

It is patently unfair that people tend to perceptually freeze an artist in a role that they will inevitably abandon as they mature. If anything, people should be impressed by such drive and talent at such a young age and only expect that talent to increase and become more refined over time. I look at it this way: Were you doing anything nearly that industrious and impressive as a teenager? Neither was I.

The initial impression people get will be a lasting one, for better or worse.

This does illustrate, however, that no matter how talented you might be, people can be illogically narrow-minded, which can harm your career down the road. I remember a job I got when I was 17; everyone I worked with was in their 30s. Even when I finally reached 30, they still viewed me as a 17-year-old. Quite frankly, it really annoyed me and damaged any credibility I might have otherwise had if they had met me years later. Meanwhile, in other professional settings, people who met me as an adult viewed me differently, and treated me with more respect.

What can be learned from this? If you are a young person looking to go into a high-profile creative endeavor that will expose you to vast numbers of people, be advised that the initial impression these people get will be a lasting one, for better or worse. I don't intend to dissuade anyone from pursuing their dream, simply to provide information that may not have previously been considered.

Benefits of Starting Young in the Entertainment Industry

There are, however, some advantages to starting a career in your youth. The most obvious is that you get a head start on building the foundation for your career. While your peers may be consumed with the latest social drama at school, you may be performing in front of thousands of people. While they're reading celebrity gossip columns, you could be learning valuable lessons about your chosen industry and how to improve your performance skills. By making your mistakes early, you can learn from them and achieve success earlier.

Another potential benefit to starting early is that adults in any given industry are often more willing to help a kid or a teenager who shows talent and initiative than they are to assist someone their own age. They can see themselves in an aspiring young person and tend to be more willing to reach down the career ladder to give a hand up to a younger person than to an adult. They're also more forgiving and ready to make allowances for someone who is younger. This can be a good time to take chances and be more experimental, when there is less at stake and you can more easily recover from mistakes because you're not out there as a professional in your field, yet. It can also be a great time to network because busy professionals will be more likely to take your calls. They might even have kids your age and would want others to treat their own children kindly, if they were calling with career questions.

What If You're Already an Adult?

All of this having been said, what can you do if you're older and trying to get into a new field? In some ways, it can be more difficult because people typically have higher expectations of their peers. On the bright side, however, you have a completely different set of circumstances than a teenager. You have been out in the real world and learned skills that can help you present yourself in a confident and professional manner. Use these skills to your advantage to make sure any first impression you make is a good one.

At this point in your life, you have tried various things and learned from them, which has helped you refine your natural talents. Skills such as being a good listener who can process information and use it to effectively sell to others can suddenly become invaluable when you're trying to promote yourself and network within your chosen industry.

For those of you with a bit more wear on your tires than some of my younger readers, I feel your pain. I have heard many creative people who achieved tremendous success at a young age comment that, because they achieved success so early in life without years or even decades of struggle, they were under the impression that everyone reached their creative goals with relative ease. Facing such attitudes and preconceptions, when you've been working endlessly while making very little career headway, can be extremely frustrating and, sometimes, even insulting. Not everyone gets fabulous career breaks so it can be hard to feel like you're perpetually sitting on the sidelines watching everyone else enjoy the action when you never get a chance to get in the game. Just remember that your success will be even sweeter when you finally do achieve it.

CHAPTER 8

Building Your Credentials

Not All Experts Are Created Equal

Becoming an actual expert in any field takes hard work. While there are many who claim to be experts, there is no substitute for hard work and experience. If you can't hold your own with experts in your field, you're not there yet. Real experts can't be easily fooled, and being pretentious can actually harm your reputation. To be a credible expert, you need to have good answers to tough questions and know effective strategies and techniques in your field that the average person doesn't know. Simply stating the obvious will only make someone look amateurish.

**The more media coverage you get,
the more you *can* get.**

How can expertise be attained? Constantly challenge yourself, learn as much as you can from people established in your field, and actively participate in your field. Learning from your own mistakes and the mistakes of other professionals in your industry is a very effective way to develop your expertise.

Credentials are very important as you promote yourself. While you certainly may have a natural talent, strengthening your credentials will make you more attractive to potential clients and customers and to the media because those credentials present you as an authority and give you increased credibility.

As you look to build your press coverage, credentials become increasingly critical as you try to reach higher levels of media. If you look at the publicity equation from a journalist's point of view, the importance becomes clear. Consider what you would do if you were a journalist and your editor wanted you to write a story about a musician. Which of the following profiles would look more appealing to both you and the editor?

Musician 1

- Has been performing for 5 years
- Started as a backup musician for major recording artists
- Recognized by a national magazine as a top-ten artist last year
- Sold over 250,000 albums
- Toured America and England last summer to sold-out crowds
- Was recently interviewed by America's #1 music magazine

Musician 2

- Has been performing for 5 years
- Recently released an independent album
- Has an active social media page
- Was recently interviewed by a local newspaper

If a journalist is considering interviewing one of the two musicians above, the first musician will be the one to get the interview because accomplishments significantly improve how someone will be perceived by the media and the public. Be sure to list your credentials on your website, press releases, and other appropriate promotional materials. They let customers and the media know that they're dealing with a professional.

Improving Your Credentials

So what can you do if you don't already have impressive credentials? Start building them right away. If you are working in a profession that requires university degrees or industry certifications for career advancement, start working on attaining the qualifications you'll need.

Academic qualifications are more important for some professions than others. Obviously, if you want to be a surgeon, you'll need a very specific program of education and degrees for that profession. In some artistic fields, however, actual experience is more important than university degrees. When I used to audition for rock bands, I was never once asked about my educational background. It simply didn't matter because it was my talent that had to stand on its own, not my academic achievements.

When considering ways to promote your credentials, think of things you have done professionally in your field. Where has your work appeared or been reviewed? If you're a performer, where have you played? What kinds of awards and recognition have you received? Where have you gotten media coverage? Have you done any public speaking about what you do professionally?

I cannot emphasize the importance of credentials enough. After my many years of working in PR, it is abundantly clear that credentials alone can often be the primary deciding factor in whether a journalist decides to do a story about someone. *Wanting* to be an expert or accomplished professional in a field doesn't make it so. There are simply no substitutes for experience and actual accomplishments.

Now, having said all of that, there are certain credentials you can acquire relatively quickly, or at least more quickly than by getting a college degree in a subject. The effectiveness of these credentials depends largely on the profession. For example, if you are a painter, the number and prominence of shows and galleries that have featured your work will likely be far more important than the university you attended, unless you went to a particularly prestigious university. Aside from that, however, your work and how well recognized it is will be the most important factors.

If you are a musician, music journalists will be impressed by the well-known and respected musicians with whom you work, the types of venues you play, the size of crowds you draw, the music media outlets that cover you, and the number of units you sell. In music, those are the credentials that matter.

It's far better to make your mistakes in front of a small audience than a large one.

Getting street cred in your field is a process that takes time. Think of it as building a house. You start off with the foundation, which is the smaller venues and press outlets. You might begin by showing your work at local galleries that are only covered by regional newspapers. Don't be discouraged by smaller-scale coverage because every time you are interviewed, you are improving your interview skills. It's far better to make your mistakes in front of a small audience than a large one.

Once you have been interviewed by your local media, you will have something to add to your credentials. Journalists and producers like to see that you have been interviewed before. It lets them know that you have experience with the process so you are more likely to be a good interviewee. Additionally, seeing that you have been interviewed by other media outlets signals to journalists and producers that their peers have found you interesting enough and professional enough to interview. It is a sort of unspoken endorsement. Remember, the more media coverage you get, the more you *can* get.

How Credentials Differentiate You From the Competition

Having strong credentials can not only help you build your media profile but also increase your sales. Imagine an art gallery that lists upcoming shows in an email newsletter that is sent to existing customers, if the following two listings appear, which artist do you think will have a better turnout?

Artist 1
This artist has been painting for 15 years and recently won the regional award for her latest watercolor collection. She is a top-selling artist at the gallery and a frequent speaker at the city's annual fine art conference. She has a B.A. in Fine Art.

Artist 2
This artist has been painting for 15 years, and this is her first show. She has a B.A. in Fine Art.

The first artist will likely have a bigger turnout simply because of her proven track record of success. When potential customers see the two listings, they will be drawn to the first one because it comes across as more professional. Even if they have never heard of that artist before, they will be impressed by her credentials.

There is a perception that the first artist is more talented because of her accomplishments and recognition within the art industry. In truth, the second artist may very well be more talented than the first artist, but the first one is the more successful marketer. Fairly or unfairly, customer perceptions are tremendously important in business and can have a dramatic effect on your sales.

Fairly or unfairly, customer perceptions are tremendously important in business and can have a dramatic effect on your sales.

Keep in mind that anything which presents you in a more professional light will improve your credentials. Investigate what the most successful people in your field are doing and work toward similar achievements in your own career.

CHAPTER 9

Doing What You Can With What You Have

Finding Your Target Market

As you approach various opportunities, it is important to remember that, in creative fields, there is much more subjectivity than in some other fields, such as science and math. Because of this, you could ask ten different people what they think of your work and get ten different answers. This is why getting exposure to professionals in your chosen field *and* members of the general public is very important. As you get more exposure, you'll start to notice trends, such as specific traits shared by people who enjoy your work.

Keep in mind that there are many different markets for artistic wares so there is plenty of room for all sorts of artists. As you see trends emerge from your observations about people who enjoy your work, use that information to advance your career by finding out more about these people. They will likely be your target market.

Your **target market** is the group of prospects and customers you want to aim your marketing activities at because this group contains the people who are most likely to buy what you're selling. By observing their shared traits, where they spend their time, and what activities they enjoy, you can better target your marketing activities to ensure that your message reaches your target market. I'll discuss how to identify and reach your target market in more detail in chapter 11.

Being in the Place That's Right for You

As your awareness of your customers and prospects increases, you will more effectively be able to make decisions that will move your career in the desired direction. This is important because it will help you discern which opportunities to pursue and which to avoid. For example, if you are a heavy metal vocalist, you probably wouldn't want to bother auditioning for *American Idol* or *The X Factor* because those shows cater to a market that is very different from your target market. Fortunately, there are multitudinous ways to enter the industry.

I have seen many such television contestants lament that their dream of having a singing career is over because they didn't get through the first round of auditions. It's important to remember, however, that a TV talent show is only one of many avenues to success. Rock and pop singers have had successful careers for decades, before these televised talent shows existed, and the vast majority of rock and pop singers didn't find success through talent shows. There is no need to worry because there are plenty of opportunities out there, and just because you don't get one gig doesn't mean you won't get others.

These shows are looking for a very specific type of singer. By the very nature of such programs, loads of very talented singers who don't fit that cookie-cutter mold will be rejected. It doesn't mean, however, that all of those people aren't talented, it just means they might be better-suited for *different* singing gigs. Just think of all the legendary artists with distinct vocal styles who probably wouldn't have made the cut on *American Idol* and *The X Factor*. So many have been hugely successful, despite not having the kind of voice that would fit into the televised talent show format in which the judges are seeking a very specific type of voice. It's just like the difference between a theatrical

Broadway singer and a rock singer. They may both have fantastic voices, but they will appeal to different audiences. Neither one is better than the other, they're simply different.

On balance, there are also plenty of people who don't make it through simply because they can't sing well. This is why it's important to get feedback from many professionals and look at the trend of their aggregate opinions. Having an accurate sense of reality is of paramount importance when assessing your talent in any creative field.

As with the example of the singers, if you are a traditional painter in the style of Renoir, an avant-garde gallery that specializes in abstract works verging on the bizarre won't be the right place to try to get your work shown. You would want to direct your efforts toward getting your paintings in front of *your* target market. There is a market for your work, you just need to find it.

The Power of Reinvention and Longevity

In creative fields, it's common to see a flavor-of-the-month taking out the latest top contender. Once knocked out of the spotlight, it can be tremendously difficult to achieve career longevity. But, for those who are very creative and business savvy, reinvention can lead to a long and successful career and a lifetime of respectable income.

As an example of successful image transition, consider Dee Snider, the lead singer and songwriter from the popular eighties metal band Twisted Sister. Clearly, any career transition after having such a wild and flamboyant stage persona was going to take some clever strategy because that persona presented such a strong brand. Snider wisely positioned himself as a skilled host, eventually becoming a VH-1 regular. Over the years, he has racked up numerous credentials: rock star, songwriter, TV show host, radio personality, actor, screenwriter, reality TV star, voice-over artist, and author. He even penned a Christmas song that was recorded by Celine Dion. While many of his heavy metal contemporaries have faded into obscurity, Snider has maintained longevity in the entertainment industry by reinventing himself and developing an image that will work well for him over the long run.

Another dramatic example has been that of English synthpop singer and songwriter Kim Wilde. Her reinvention from an eighties pop star to an award-winning garden designer, featured celebrity on major UK gardening shows, and successful gardening author has brought her tremendous success in a completely different career realm. Now that's some pretty impressive reinvention.

Perhaps the finest example of successful image reinvention is former *Partridge Family* star Danny Bonaduce. He has truly reinvented himself from a child actor to a successful radio personality, talk-show host, television presenter, celebrity boxing and wrestling champ, author, and reality TV star, which is no small feat when you look at the scores of child stars before and after him who never successfully made such a transition. Additionally, he did all of this with endearing humor and great candor.

CHAPTER 10

Considering Your Competition

What Is Differentiation?

Differentiation essentially addresses how you are different from your competitors. What makes you stand out? What distinguishes you from the other professionals in your field? What makes your products and services better than everyone else's? In order to be able to identify what differentiates you, it is critical to know what your competitors are offering.

Consider which of your competitors have the greatest amount of **market share** (the percentage of your market that each competitor serves) and why. Are they successful because of the quality of their products or services? Do they offer exceptional customer service? Is their pricing attractive to consumers?

Once you have identified what your competitors offer, consider how your business is perceived by prospects and customers. Are you able to stand out from your competitors? What are your strengths and weaknesses? It's important to be realistic in your assessment of what you can offer your customers and where your business may need improvement.

What is your competition doing today?

While the temptation to be all things to all people can be strong because a broad offering may seem like a good way to gain market share, it can actually result in a decline in sales because it undermines your focus. By concentrating on your strengths, you can focus your efforts, time, and budget on becoming the strongest in the market space that you occupy.

Keeping up With the Joneses

What is your competition doing today? How about next week or next month? It's important to be aware of your competitors' latest products, pricing, promotions, and distribution channels so you don't lose market share.

When determining your pricing, examine competitors' prices. Consider how you can compete on price by improving the efficiency of your processes and by reducing how much you have to pay for materials and equipment. For example, if you make a craft item, look at the processes that you currently use to make your crafts. Are there any steps that can be combined to shorten the amount of time spent making the items? Are there any different materials you could use that would enable you to create items more quickly, such as using hot glue instead of craft glue? Can you afford to take advantage of volume discounts by purchasing supplies in bulk?

Since lowering prices isn't always the best strategy, be aware not only of price promotions but also promotions adding value to a customer's purchase. Are your competitors offering something that you aren't, such as elevated status or excitement? Creative entrepreneurs are especially well-suited to leveraging status as an attractive selling feature. For example, if a jewelry designer's products are perceived to be exclusive, the designer may be able to increase prices and *still* increase sales.

CHAPTER 11

Defining Your Target Market

Who Is in Your Target Market?

Artists and entertainers are in business, just like manufacturers and retailers. Know your target market, serve them well, manage your finances wisely, and you can achieve success.

If everyone is in your target market, then, by definition, your market isn't targeted.

I have lost count of the number of times I have met with a new client and, when I asked who was in his or her target market, the client cheerfully replied, "Everyone!" While people certainly mean well when they give that response, they are unknowingly making life harder on themselves when it comes to marketing. If everyone is in your target market, then, by definition, your market isn't targeted. Even when examining sales of products that everyone uses, such as tissues, different companies will have different target markets. There will be some companies aiming for customers who seek products primarily on the basis of price, as well as those targeting customers who seek premium products of a higher quality.

As I stated in chapter 9, your target market is the group of people most likely to want to buy your products or services. It is essentially the demographic group that you are aiming your promotional activities toward, since that group will be most interested in buying what you are selling. It is literally the market you are targeting.

As you try to define your target market, consider the kinds of people most likely to appreciate and buy your products or services. For example, if you design clothing that is reminiscent of the Elizabethan era, getting your message in front of customers who typically buy tailored suits wouldn't make much sense. It would be a waste of your valuable time and money. Instead, you'd have more success trying to get your message in front of people who are interested in Renaissance fairs because they would be more likely to buy from you. What kinds of magazines and websites do these people like? What radio stations do they listen to? Which TV shows do they watch? By getting your message into those media outlets, through paid advertising, press coverage, or both, you will be effectively reaching out to an audience that will be much more receptive to your message.

Reach Your Target Market Amidst the Marketplace Noise

There is a great deal of marketing noise in our everyday lives, and people have become quite good at tuning out many of the marketing messages that bombard them daily. This is why refining your methods of reaching out to prospective customers is so critical. By focusing on getting the attention of people who are already interested in the type of products or services you provide, you are reaching out to a comparatively friendly audience.

I have heard many creative entrepreneurs express concern that they might only appeal to a niche audience. Historically, we have all seen large corporations turn down certain projects based on the assumption that they appeal to too narrow a niche to be profitable. Fortunately, as the Internet continues to move the power of information and product distribution into the hands of the individual sellers, large companies are finding that they don't always know consumers as well as they claim to and, consequently, miss tremendous profit opportunities.

Why is this significant? Because it means that you can now capitalize on opportunities that would have been difficult to leverage before the Internet became widely used. You can find seemingly obscure target markets and get your message in front of them, which can result in sales. As online communication and social networking continue to improve and the barriers to entry in professional distribution fall away, many creative entrepreneurs no longer need the approval of corporate types who once wielded the power of determining who would live and die in the marketplace. These days, it's much easier to be your own boss. With the right skills, talent, and drive, you can create your own success.

Whether you make gothic furniture, modernist sculpture, historically accurate costumes for re-enactors, or pillows embroidered with Hungarian sayings, there is a market for you. Customers are looking for your goods and services so it's important to get your message in front of them. There are plenty of websites that successfully sell not only these types of products but lots of others that would appeal to more narrow markets.

People can't buy a product or service if they don't know it exists.

There are markets for all kinds of products, and high sales can be achieved, if a strong message is presented to a well-targeted market. There is no wizardry to this method. Good quality can sell itself, *if* people know it is available. Therein lies a major factor that stops many an otherwise successful entrepreneur. People can't buy a product or service if they don't know it exists. Additionally, there is a segment of the market that will be *more* likely to buy certain products and services than other segments. The challenge is in finding the segment of people who are *most* likely to be interested in buying what you're selling.

To ensure that you understand your target market, ask your existing customers questions. These are the folks who were interested enough to buy from you, and there are many more people out there just like them. Those who have already made purchases can tell you what finally persuaded them to make a purchase and whether there were specific reasons they didn't buy immediately. By keeping an open dialogue with consumers, you can learn valuable information about what they like best and what they want more of. This kind of detailed information is any marketer's dream.

Value is *always* determined by the buyer, not the seller.

Learning what customers like, don't like, and want is only helpful if you act on this information. Simply knowing it and continuing to conduct business in the same way achieves nothing. To maximize your sales potential, it is important to sell what customers want, not simply a narrow selection of what you think they *should* want. As sellers, we must always remember that value is *always* determined by the buyer, not the seller.

CHAPTER 12

Customer Service

The Significance of Customer Service

An incredibly important part of any business, regardless of the size, is customer service. Whether you own a huge international retailer or you're a solo entrepreneur selling your own line of custom clothing designs, treating your customers well is of paramount importance. A happy customer will tell everyone they know about how well they've been treated. That customer will be an advocate for your business, which is an asset in a world in which word-of-mouth recommendations go a long way. Additionally, a happy customer is far more likely to be brand loyal and buy from you again.

When customers speak . . . listen. They might only tell you once. Sometimes, they won't tell you with words but with their actions. This is a recurrent scenario I frequently see on the TV reality show *Ramsay's Kitchen Nightmares*. Time and again, restaurant owners deep in debt and desperate for customers declare to internationally successful chef and business owner Gordon Ramsay that their customers never complain about the restaurant's food so it must be good. The thing is that customers generally *don't* bother complaining because they assume nothing will be changed on the basis of their complaint. Also, many people feel uncomfortable being confrontational so they simply don't make subsequent purchases after having a bad experience. Worse yet, they often tell their friends who then also avoid the seller. Being aware of how best to serve your customers is just as important for a musician or an artist as it is for the CEO of a major corporation or a restaurant owner.

Create a Survey to Learn What Customers Want

I often hear clients wonder aloud, "What do customers want?" My answer is simply, "Ask them." Believe me, customers are not shy about giving you their opinions, if you ask. While they generally won't offer unsolicited opinions, when prompted, they will tell you the good and the bad points about your business. Being on the receiving end of such feedback may sometimes leave you feeling a bit vulnerable and hurt, but it should also help you to feel empowered and proactive because you are strong enough to face honest criticism and take steps to provide even better customer service.

Getting new customers is significantly more expensive than retaining existing customers so time and money spent finding out how to satisfy, and even delight, your existing customers is certainly well spent. It can pay off tremendously by helping you increase your sales. Whether you use a traditional written survey or an online survey, the methods of ensuring that you get useful information are the same. Below are tips that will make your survey more successful:

How can you get people to take time to fill out a survey?

While people don't mind giving their opinions, they are very busy. An effective way to persuade them to take the time to fill out a survey is to offer some kind of reward for completion. You could offer a coupon for a discount on a future purchase, a gift certificate, or a sweepstakes entry for a bigger prize.

Make your survey questions clear and concise.

The longer your survey is, the less likely people will take the time to complete it. It is important to get a high response rate because that will give you more information to use in determining how to improve your business. Keep the survey questions brief and simple.

Make sure you can use the information you get.

If you write a survey asking customers to evaluate your customer service, you not only want to know how it rates, but why. Knowing about customer approval or disapproval without knowing specifically why customers feel that way won't help you make the necessary changes.

For example, if customers rate your company's customer service as "poor," you'll need to know why so you know what to improve. Are customers dissatisfied because they're being kept on hold too long? Is it because you don't offer a next-day shipping option? Are you making it too difficult for them to return products that were damaged in shipping? Unless you follow up on that survey question by asking why customers gave a certain rating, you'll only get partial information that is difficult to use effectively.

Expect the unexpected.

At the end of your survey, have a blank space where people can provide comments on issues you may not have asked about in the survey questions. This section of the survey can often be the most revealing because you will learn about unexpected problem areas you can correct. Additionally, you'll often receive compliments about your company's strengths, which are always nice to hear.

Once you have valuable feedback information from a survey, be sure to use it to improve your customer service. Regularly surveying customers can be an incredibly effective tool in your marketing arsenal.

CHAPTER 13

Building Brand Equity

What Is Brand Equity?

Brand equity is essentially the value that your brand name has when compared to competitors. While it's not easy to measure with great accuracy, it can make a huge difference to your bottom line.

To better understand brand equity, imagine two competing companies making basically the same products, such as leather handbags. If you compared the companies' products and found them to be equal in all respects, such as quality, features, size, and function, it would instinctively be reasonable to assume that the prices would also be about the same. This is where brand equity kicks in and makes a huge difference in how customers perceive a company's products.

If one of the handbag companies is recognized as having a premium brand with a powerful reputation, the cost of its bags may be hundreds of dollars more than its competitors, for no reason other than the value that customers see in that particular brand. A recognizable brand that has a favorable image and is known for its quality and prestige can command a higher price in the marketplace, even when there are comparable products of the same quality available for a lower price.

Your image goes hand in hand with your brand equity, which plays a significant role in determining the amount of revenue you can earn. Working to build your brand equity is most effective when you use several approaches at once to develop and strengthen your reputation. Paid advertising, free publicity, brand-focused marketing materials and packaging, social media . . . use it all.

Standing Out From the Crowd

I often tell my clients that I don't make the rules about how people get press coverage, I just follow them. I look at the process as an obstacle course through which I have to maneuver in order to get press coverage for my clients. I frequently hear people express their frustration with media outlets that will feature an "expert" in some sort of vague field, instead of a guest with a solid professional background in the subject who can provide information that is actually rooted in substance. Generally, a huge component in determining who gets booked for an interview is brand equity.

> **There are ways you can differentiate yourself so you stand out from the competition.**

While there may be many other professionals who can address or present the same issues that you can, there are ways you can differentiate yourself so you stand out from the competition. In doing this, you build and strengthen your own brand, which helps you gain more business and publicity.

A perfect example of the differentiation that leads to strong brand equity is homemaking icon Martha Stewart. The subjects she addresses certainly aren't unique or revolutionary in any way. She is simply doing what hundreds of enterprising women have done for decades, by sharing tips on cooking, entertaining, and decorating. This is not a new concept, yet Stewart successfully created tremendous demand for her brand.

What makes her so different from all of the other domestic divas out there? She presents her products and ideas in a very high-end manner. She doesn't just buy the ingredients she uses in her recipes, she also grows them. She has built an empire by presenting her wares with an understated sophistication that transforms mundane domesticity into an elegant art form.

Considering the space that Stewart occupies in the marketplace, how could an aspiring homemaking expert differentiate herself from Stewart to effectively compete in the marketplace? A competing homemaker could focus her message on time-saving and money-saving tips, in contrast to Stewart's more time-consuming and expensive projects. This approach could help the competitor occupy the same general space in the market, yet appeal to a different segment of that homemaking market.

Additionally, competitors would need to fully understand the power of Stewart's finely tuned brand. With many providers of homemaking advice and tools on the market, why do so many customers decide to purchase goods branded with Martha Stewart's name rather than those of a competitor? The distinction is the strength in her company's brand equity. There is the appeal of quality and sophistication because products are presented in a very traditional and upscale manner. Consumers hope that by buying these products and following Stewart's advice, their homes will look as inviting and cozy as those pictured in her magazines and books.

Does Your Image Fit What You're Selling?

Among the various issues that demand attention from creative entrepreneurs is the consideration of image building. Your brand is very much tied into your public image and can translate into a dramatic increase, or decrease, in sales.

Job seekers are used to thinking in these terms when interviewing for employment. People know that wearing a suit to an interview for a high-level position at a financial institution will project a professional image to a prospective employer.

Sometimes, however, creative entrepreneurs are challenged by trying to create an image that will appeal to a target market, particularly if that market has yet to be defined. It is important to build an image that is a good fit for your particular business.

Will Prospects Perceive You the Way You Want Them To?

Whether you're a jewelry designer selling your wares at craft shows, a writer trying to sell books at seminars, or a musician promoting your music downloads and gigs online, it is important that the image you project meets the expectations of prospective customers. While it shouldn't matter, it unfortunately does. Further, it can be surprising how many conclusions people jump to based solely on image.

A perfect example of this can be seen on popular TV talent shows such as *American Idol* and *The X Factor*, where the judges often comment on having been surprised by a singer's talent after initially being put off by the singer's clothing or demeanor. Before even hearing one note, the judges make all sorts of assumptions based solely on appearance. The same thing happens all the time in the marketplace. An awareness of your image is critical to managing how it affects your business.

Does Your Brand Reflect How Customers Want to Be Seen?

Interestingly, the image customers want to project to define *themselves* plays a huge role in branding. For example, the high-end handbag manufacturers I mentioned earlier appeal directly to their high-income customers by presenting an image of quality and luxury. Products are shown in glossy ads that project sophisticated style. At some point, the retail cost of the product far exceeds the cost of materials and advertising.

Your brand is much like a mirror that is being held up to your customers.

What enables manufacturers to charge extortionately high prices for these goods is completely a result of branding. Customers recognize that these bags are only affordable by a small percentage of the market, which in turn drives their appeal. The exclusivity of the bags and their sophisticated image are therefore transferred to the customers who are seen with them. If a brand doesn't project the image its target market expects to see, sales will decrease accordingly.

Brand equity is so important that companies work very hard to protect their brands. In the handbag example, people want to be seen with these designer bags because they convey an image of wealth and glamour. Such a desire and demand from consumers who can't afford expensive handbags, but want the image these brands convey, drives the counterfeit market in which imitations of the designer brands are sold at much cheaper prices.

When counterfeit goods are sold for a fraction of the retail cost and anyone can look like they're carrying one of these signature products, suddenly, they are no longer viewed as exclusive, and wealthy customers lose interest because the products are now seen as common. This is bad news to the high-end manufacturer who wants the brand to remain exclusive so it can continue to warrant a high price. For this reason, the designers actively pursue counterfeiters who undermine their hard-won brand equity.

As you think about building your own brand equity, think about what kind of image you want to project. Do you want to be seen as serious and businesslike or funny and casual? Do you want to have a rockin' image or a straitlaced image?

It is important to develop a brand that not only projects you in a positive light, but also reflects how your customers want to see themselves. In some ways, your brand is much like a mirror that is being held up to your customers so they can make sure that they are presenting themselves to the world in the way they want to be seen.

Does Your Marketing Express the Level of Value You Want to Communicate?

Your communication with buyers in the market is critical. Everything from your website to your product packaging speaks volumes about how you run your business. Whether consciously or subconsciously, customers absorb this information and it affects their purchasing decisions.

Take a look at the packaging and promotional materials from various companies. Notice that expensive products seen as high-end luxury items are packaged accordingly. They will often come in heavier packaging that is glossy and expensive-looking, in keeping with the product's image. They often feature details such as embossed lettering or gold foil. Marketing brochures representing these products are often glossy, four-color brochures on a heavier weight paper. Likewise, cheap items will often be in more flimsy packaging made of lower-grade materials. The quality of the product is apparent simply by looking at the packaging.

As a consumer, before you even open the packaging, you have started making assumptions about what's inside, based solely on the external appearance. People do the same thing every day as they encounter various businesses. Whether they're right or wrong, first impressions contribute greatly to people's purchasing decisions and their perceptions of your brand, which can have a significant effect on profitability. Awareness of customer expectations in all marketing functions can be a highly effective way to increase sales and retain customers.

CHAPTER 14

Brand Equity and Fame

Building Your Brand Equity

With the advent of reality TV and nationally televised talent shows that promise everything from cash to record deals, the Western world worships at the altar of television. Media is king and everyone wants to be a star in their field or, in some cases, *any* field. Because of this, the competition for media coverage is fierce. No matter how far you get in your field, there is always a long line of people standing behind you who will be more than happy to take your place should you fail.

What separates the big names from unknowns is brand equity. As stated in the previous chapter, it is the power and worth of a name, whether it's a person's name or the name of a company or organization. Think about any product category. Who are the industry leaders in the soft drink industry, the software industry, or the auto industry? If we asked a group of people to name names, we'd likely hear the same names over and over. That's because these companies have strong brand equity.

As a person in a creative industry, your public image will be very important and will contribute greatly to how people, and potential customers, perceive you. How do you want to present yourself to the world? Will you select a persona that will serve you well over the long term? Selecting an avant-garde persona can be an effective way to get attention, but that very same persona can shorten your shelf life. Starting off as a young person, it's easy to think you'll be young and hip forever, but age gets all of us, and what looks cool for a twenty-three-year-old may look decidedly uncool for someone in their forties.

Consider the carefully crafted image of goth rocker Marilyn Manson, who rose to musical prominence in the nineties. Manson was a brilliant marketer and knew how to present an image that would shock parents and attract young rock fans in equal measure. There's just one catch: How can someone still pull off that image in their forties? It's difficult.

In contrast, look at Brian Setzer, the front man of the eighties rockabilly band The Stray Cats. He seamlessly evolved into a very sustainable image that allows for graceful aging when he formed the Brian Setzer Orchestra, which quickly gained popularity performing jump blues and swing.

If you are not an entertainer, you will likely have more leeway, but it is still important to create an image that can grow and evolve with your business. As a creative entrepreneur, you are essentially your own brand. If you carefully manage your brand, you can build strong brand equity that can serve you well for years to come.

The Potential Hazards of Reality Television

Reality TV is a great example of the power of television to advance or, indeed, even create a career for someone who was previously unknown to the general public. While it can be an effective vehicle to gain quick fame, the fame is rarely long-lasting. I have heard countless reality TV stars proclaim that they will maintain a solid career in television long after their season ends, but very few actually accomplish this.

Why are these forays into celebrity so brief? The primary reason is because the reality TV star has essentially become famous on the back of the show's brand equity, not his or her own. Therein lies the problem with maintaining any sort of regular fan base. If viewers are fans of the show itself, they are less concerned with the various interchangeable faces they see from season to season and more interested in the actual mechanics of the show. This is a problem for any reality TV star looking to extend their time in the spotlight.

How can you do this? Part of the answer lies in the foundation you build for your career. What do you do? What do you sell? If you are a musician, then you sell music. If you are a painter, then you sell paintings. If you are a reality TV star, however, what do you sell? It would be inaccurate to say that you sell entertainment because the show is unscripted. That means your function on the show is neither as a writer nor an actor. That's not to say you can't do those things apart from the show, but you're not getting the opportunity to display your actual talent *on* the show. That presents a problem. How can you get your creative talents in front of people, especially at a time when you have the attention of a huge audience?

Thankfully, with the popularity of social media, you have a greatly increased chance of people visiting your various sites online. How will you keep them coming back, though, once the show is over and you're no longer at the forefront of their minds? There is a tremendous amount of truth in the saying, "Out of sight, out of mind." Making regular appearances on a current TV show is tantamount to having regular advertisements on television that remind the viewing public that you're out there. People get busy, however, and other things catch their attention. Once you're no longer on a show, people quickly move onto other things.

If you are going to be on a reality TV show and want to build a fan base, you need to have an Internet presence and completed products available for sale before or during the show's first airing. It is important to act while viewers' interest is at its highest point. Waiting until the show is in reruns might still get you some traffic, but it will be significantly less because the novelty of the show has cooled and most regular viewers have already seen it.

The same is true for performers who experience a revival in interest because of a where-are-they-now type of TV appearance. I remember when actor, musician, and seventies teen idol Leif Garrett was on VH1's *Behind the Music*, after years out of the national spotlight. It seemed as if VH1 aired that episode incessantly and, instantly, all of the dormant Leif Garrett fans across the US sprang to life. Garrett suddenly found himself as a guest on other programs and his fan base was once again connected and tuned into his activities. It was the kind of publicity revival a performer could only dream of.

Garrett did leverage the opportunity from a marketing standpoint, but the impact and profitability could have been so much greater if he'd had original songs recorded and ready for purchase when all the publicity hit. As with any kind of marketing, you want to make sure you have a strong message and available products *before* you get people's attention so that, when you finally get in front of them, you don't miss a valuable opportunity to sell and stay connected for future marketing efforts and sales.

You may be a creative person with no desire to be on a reality TV show, yet you may get some sort of press coverage in print, online, or on TV that brings you sudden attention. The same rules apply in that it will be a fleeting moment of fame, unless you take advantage of that attention and turn it into a business opportunity so that you're not simply yesterday's news.

The Role of Fame in Your Career

We live in a culture that worships celebrity to an exaggerated degree. Celebrity can certainly be a useful tool, but it is no substitute for substance. If fame is your sole objective, you will very likely be surprised to eventually discover the unexpected emptiness and loneliness it can bring. Sure, fame looks glamorous from the outside, but that doesn't make it substantial. Just as artificial flavors, food coloring, and fancy packaging might make a dessert look appealing, it isn't necessarily delicious or nutritious. Appearances can be very misleading.

Fame is essentially a form of brand equity but, when it becomes the primary or even the only objective, it is no longer simply a means to an end of building a creative business. It becomes the end itself.

Having fame without money can quickly become a nightmare.

Fame can certainly help you sell your products and services, however. As it differentiates you from your competitors, it also drives demand for your offerings and enables you to sell more products or services and possibly even charge higher prices.

Over the years, I have worked with many people whose career goals consisted of nothing more than acquiring sudden fame. Many of these people actually did achieve their dreams of being interviewed by radio personalities, print journalists, and TV hosts. For networking and marketing purposes, it can certainly sound impressive to be able to refer to your latest media interview, but will that generate income over the long term? Those who have no other marketing activities in place generally discover the huge flaw in their plans . . . how will they make money and build a solid career doing something they enjoy?

Being interviewed by the media is a great way to get your name out in the public marketplace but, if you have nothing to sell or promote, you're most likely burning up a lot of time and not bringing in much, if any, revenue. Such a situation isn't sustainable for an entrepreneur.

Additionally, having fame without money can quickly become a nightmare. Just imagine being recognized everywhere you go, without having enough money to maintain a buffer zone of distance from the gaze of the public to protect your privacy and, frankly, your sanity.

CHAPTER 15

Where Do I Start?

Determining What You Already Have

In the marketing classes I have taught to creative entrepreneurs over the years, this is the part people have always told me they find the most intimidating. My goal is to make this as simple as possible and provide you with the tools that will enable you to create your own personalized evaluation of your business so you can see how it relates to the competition within your field. By going through this process of realistic assessment, you will be better able to see opportunities that can help you to get your own business off the ground.

How to Create an *Analysis of Resources*

To start, you should take a look at the resources you already have by using the ***Analysis of Resources*** process that follows. The reason for this is so that you can clearly see what resources you can begin using right away, if you aren't using them already. In my experience, I have found that once people go through this exercise, they usually discover that they have more available resources than they realized, which is good news.

ANALYSIS OF RESOURCES

This section of the plan documents your credentials and experience by examining what you have already achieved in your field. It is important to be aware of these factors because they are critical not only to how you are able to function in your business, but also because of their impact on the media and prospective customers.

Additionally, this section examines what resources you have available to help advance your career. As an entrepreneur, it is important to be aware of every tool available for you to use as you work toward success. By completing this analysis, you can see just how much you already have in your favor.

Credentials

Here, you list any degrees or certifications that you have. Be sure to include any pertinent career levels you have achieved that are within your field.

Experience

Think about what you have done that relates to this endeavor. What experience do you already have that can help you get from where you are now to where you want to be?

Directly Related Skills

If you're a singer, have you done any performances or have you been hired to perform backing vocals on someone else's recording project? If you're a crafter or a woodworker, have you sold any of your work? If you're a painter or sculptor, has your work been featured in any galleries?

Indirectly Related Skills

If you want to be a professional painter and you have reached the level of marketing manager in your corporate day job, include that in this section. While experience in marketing doesn't contribute to your painting ability, it will be a huge advantage that can help you sell your work and build your brand equity. If you've done work writing professionally or have worked in sales, that will also be a tremendous help as you build your business because those skills can contribute to your creative business.

Achievements

In this section, list any awards or business recognition you have achieved. This will be useful in your marketing materials because it will distinguish you from amateurs. Achievements within your industry establish you as a credible professional within your field. Including these in your marketing materials will enable you to present yourself in a favorable light so you can put forth a positive first impression to the public. These are also important to tell the media about because the more successful you are, the more likely the media are to cover what you're doing.

Resources

It is critical to have a clear picture of exactly what resources you have available. Resources can be a huge expense so the more you already have, the better. Consider all of the tools, assistance from others, and funding you currently have that can help you achieve your goals. By completing this section you can see what you have and what you still need to acquire.

Staff

Typically, entrepreneurs in creative fields are starting out on their own with no employees. If you are the only one working on your business, simply state that here. If there are others helping you, however, note that here also. While you may not be at the level where you can afford to hire employees, yet, regular assistance from friends and family members does count. When even a small group of people work hard together toward the same goal, they can achieve amazing things.

Write down the names of those helping you in your business and, next to each, describe specifically what that person is doing within your business. For example, if you are handling the creation of products and your best friend is in charge of public relations, stating those essentially "filled" positions in this section shows you what you already have and what other help you'll need. As you get more assistance, whether through family and friends or through employees, add those names and functions here so you can see the human resources of your growing business at a glance.

Products

If you sell a tangible product, instead of or in addition to a service, list here what inventory you have that is already completed and ready to sell. The reason services aren't listed here is because they don't require raw materials or storage space, and they don't necessitate shipping costs. Physical inventory, on the other hand, has hard costs that must be considered.

Network

Strategic networking can create business opportunities that you might not otherwise attain. Think of people you know in your field who you know well enough to contact to discuss and develop business opportunities. Are there other people within your industry who you should get to know better? Think about where you strategically need to place yourself to forge business relationships with other high-profile people in your field. There is a great deal of truth in the old saying that it's not *what* you know but *who* you know.

Additionally, are there people not in but around your field who you already know who would make strong strategic contacts? For example, if you know people in the media or in advertising, they might be helpful contacts for promotion and business opportunities.

Skills

In this section, you list your skills and talents. These are resources that can help you advance your career in any creative field.

Physical Business Space

If you have any physical space for your business, whether it's an office in which you can hold meetings with clients, a warehouse for your merchandise, or simply a small storage facility, list that here. This will be more important for businesses that sell physical products and have a great deal of in-person interaction with clients.

Funding

How much money do you realistically have available to spend on building your business? While the old saying goes that it takes money to make money, the acquisition of financial resources has gotten many entrepreneurs into serious debt so be extremely judicious with money and how you attain it. Make wise and well-researched spending decisions to avoid getting into debt or getting into a contract that is a bad deal for you. Consulting with an attorney before signing a contract is a good idea.

Reputation

Your reputation within your field can contribute greatly to your brand equity, which affects your business opportunities. Do you have name recognition in your industry? If so, are you a respected professional among your peers?

Equipment

Any equipment you have that is used in your business should be listed here. Depending on your particular business, this could include things such as computers, recording equipment, video editing equipment, a sewing machine, fabrics, paints and brushes, wood carving tools, or hot glue guns.

Distribution Channel

This is the channel through which you can sell your products and/or services. Do you sell your products yourself? Do you have established relationships with other businesses that will sell your products or services? If you do, list those here.

Platform

A platform is essentially a place to get continued exposure to your target market. This can be achieved online through a website, a blog, an ezine, an Internet radio show, a strong social media page, a podcast, etc. A local TV show would also be an excellent platform, as long as it airs regularly so you can build an audience that will hear your message on a relatively frequent basis.

The development of a successful platform requires a commitment of regular attention from you or a member of your staff. A platform needs to be frequently updated with fresh information to keep your audience coming back. As people continue to visit your platform, they will become more familiar with you and be more likely to buy from you and tell others about the value your products and/or services provide.

To understand the value of having a platform, imagine a photographer trying to get a lot of people to visit her upcoming gallery show. Without a platform, how could she let people who are interested in her work know about this event? If she has a platform, the people who visit it are already interested in her work so they would be likely to attend, if she tells them about it. By having a regularly updated platform, the photographer can share news of her upcoming show with her existing audience.

[NOTE: For the purpose of illustration, the following *Analysis of Resources* examples use fictional names for people, products, organizations, awards, and businesses.

Any resemblance to actual people, products, organizations, awards, or businesses is coincidental.]

An Example of an *Analysis of Resources* for a Painter

Creating your own analysis is as easy as going down the list of components detailed on the previous pages and simply filling in your own information. What follows is an example of an analysis for a painter.

PAINTER'S *ANALYSIS OF RESOURCES*

Credentials

- Bachelor of Fine Arts in Painting
- Worked as an assistant curator at the XYZ Museum of Art

Experience

- **Directly Related Skills**
  - Work featured at ZYZ Gallery
  - Sells paintings at annual county art show
- **Indirectly Related Skills**
  - Worked in office equipment sales and became top salesperson at company

Achievements

- Won this year's local Artistic Excellence Award from the county art board
- Voted best painter in the city by *WXY Magazine*

Resources

- **Staff**
  - me - creating the artwork
  - Dave - public relations and direct mail
  - Tony - gallery sales and art exhibitions
- **Products**
  - Original paintings
  - Lithographs
  - Remarques
  - Copper plate etchings
- **Network**
  - Nick Taylor - local painter - friend and business associate
  - Roger Andrews - local painter - friend and business associate
  - Jeanette Fredericks - high-profile designer - need to know
  - Violet Roberts - high profile gallery owner - need to know
  - Nigel Simons - reporter for local paper - acquaintance
- **Skills**
  - Strong writing ability
  - Sales skills
  - Good public speaker
- **Physical Business Space**
  - Small storage space for paintings, prints, and supplies
  - Home studio for painting
- **Funding**
  - $2,000 self-funded
- **Reputation**
  - Known among local artists
  - Not yet known well among local art buyers
- **Equipment**
  - Computer for business and website management
  - Printer for computer
  - Scanner for computer

- Office supplies: letterhead, business cards, and printer ink
- Paints, brushes, canvases, easels

- **Distribution Channel**
  - My website
  - Through the ZYZ Gallery
  - The annual county art show
- **Platform**
  - None at the moment

An Example of an *Analysis of Resources* for a Musician

Here is another example, this time for a musician. As you can see, this format can be used for just about any creative business.

<u>MUSICIAN'S *ANALYSIS OF RESOURCES*</u>

Credentials

- Studied guitar theory at ZYZ College
- Worked as guitar teacher at local music store for 5 years

Experience

- **Directly Related Skills**
  - Occasionally work as backing vocalist at XYZ Recording Studio
  - Perform at local clubs throughout the city
- **Indirectly Related Skills**
  - Worked as an account manager at a public relations firm

Achievements

- My band was voted the best local band by listeners of the city's top radio station

Resources

- **Staff**
  - me - songwriting, playing, recording, managing the band's website
  - Karen - public relations and advertising
  - Eric - booking gigs and radio station relations
- **Products**
  - CDs
  - Digital downloads
  - Branded t-shirts
  - Branded sweatshirt jackets
  - Branded mugs
  - Posters
- **Network**
  - Rick Lewis - local guitarist - friend
  - Kate Beck - local drummer - friend
  - Steve Gray - local singer who just got signed - need to know
  - Fiona Jones - hosts radio show on local music - need to know
  - Sarah Jeffries - writer for local rock magazine - acquaintance
- **Skills**
  - Strong speaking skills and good in interviews
  - Persuasive
  - Manage business funds well
- **Physical Business Space**
  - Home office for booking gigs, interviews, etc.
  - Rehearsal space for the band
- **Funding**
  - Have $5,500 saved from recent gigs

- **Reputation**
  - Known in the immediate area on the local music scene
- **Equipment**
  - Computer for business and website management
  - Printer for computer
  - Scanner for computer
  - Office supplies such as letterhead, business cards, printer ink, etc.
  - Recording and mixing software
  - 5 microphones and stands
  - 5 pairs of headphones
- **Distribution Channel**
  - The band's website
  - Merchandise table at gigs
  - Sell through music download websites
- **Platform**
  - Internet radio show on local music

CHAPTER 16

Creating a Strong Mission Statement

Developing a Mission Statement for Your Business

Once you have completed the *Analysis of Resources*, it's time to develop a mission statement for your business. You've probably read mission statements before, since most big companies have them. Sometimes they're concise and clearly articulate the actual mission of a business and, sometimes, they are far too long and read more like a PR statement of "feel good" policies that a company promotes to look good to customers.

What makes a good mission statement? Basically, it should clearly and concisely state a company's reason for being in business. Sounds simple enough, right? If it's that simple, why do so many companies have such convoluted mission statements? The main reason is because they often lose sight of what these statements are supposed to accomplish.

A strong mission statement communicates what a company wants to achieve, its goals, and its activities. The statement may include a company's products and services, the target audience, and the area where business is conducted. It may also include information about a company's differentiating features but, whatever it states, it must do so clearly and concisely.

Why is it important to be concise? It matters because if you aren't able to concisely state what you do, you may not yet have it refined in your own mind. You should always be able to give your "elevator speech" of what your mission is. As you progress in your career, you'll be surprised how often you'll need to have that information readily available to tell prospective clients and existing customers exactly what you do. It will also help you tremendously when you communicate with the media.

As a creative entrepreneur, you may decide not to show your mission statement to the public, which is fine. The value in creating one is that it takes *you* through the critical process of evaluating your goals and intended activities to ensure that you head in the right direction. It also serves as a guide that you can use as various business opportunities come your way so you can determine which opportunities are a good fit for your business and which will take you off of your intended track.

An example of where this could make a difference comes to mind. I have heard of several instances in which young musicians trying to find success in Los Angeles take an occasional acting job when it comes along, which seems harmless enough when the bills are piling up and the rent is overdue. What happens, though, if a more high-profile acting gig comes along? Since first impressions tend to be lasting, would becoming known by the public as an actor *first* hinder someone's musical credibility with the public? Probably.

Likewise, someone who strives to be a professional actor may not be taken as seriously, if he or she first becomes famous for being a musician, then goes into acting. Are there exceptions to this? Certainly, but not many. This is a case in which a clear mission statement can be a useful guide as to whether a particular opportunity will take you too far off-course from your primary objective. Ultimately, only you can make the final decision for yourself.

While you can certainly change your mission statement, it should be pretty durable over time. If you're changing it every few months, it's not serving its intended purpose, and you don't have a solid set of goals to keep you on track.

Your mission statement should be specific because a vague mission statement won't clearly define your goals. For example, it would not be useful to have a mission statement that is nebulous, like this:

My mission is to become famous and respected in the entertainment industry.

As you can see, such a mission statement doesn't state specifically what the individual does. The importance of clarity is that it helps you get focused. In the most basic terms, a mission statement simply asserts what your business is and where it's headed.

Going through the process of creating a mission statement can also guard against the tendency to want to be all things to all customers, which can undermine your marketing efforts. Develop a strong mission statement to stay focused.

A very simplified way to think about writing a mission statement is to use the sample below:

***My mission is to* (put what you do here) *for* (what result).**

— or —

***My mission is to* (put what you do here) *for* (what group of customers).**

Here are some examples for various types of creative entrepreneurs:

My mission is to run my own art gallery, featuring my paintings and works from other local artists, to enable me to fulfill my lifelong dream of working with art and being my own boss.

My mission is to sell commercial musical entertainment with a strong visual image to an international audience of pop music fans.

My mission is to offer quality perfumes made from natural ingredients to women, internationally, through sales on my website.

My mission is to create modern jewelry designs with semiprecious beads that complement the latest high-end fashions.

My mission is to provide finely crafted custom storage solutions made of high-quality wood to local residents seeking exceptional craftsmanship.

My mission is to write sophisticated comedy and perform it for audiences in big cities across the country.

My mission is to build a reputation as a serious songwriter by writing, performing, and recording meaningful songs with a strong message for international audiences.

CHAPTER 17

Creating a *Strategic Marketing Analysis*

Analyzing and Strategizing

Once you have written a mission statement that accurately represents what you do and what your goals are, the next step is to write a ***Strategic Marketing Analysis***. By using the same marketing concepts that traditional corporations use, you can get organized and make the most of your efforts.

There are many formats for strategic plans and business plans available. These also vary according to the particular businesses to which they are applied. They can be a few pages long or voluminous, depending on the needs of the individual or organization creating them. For the purposes of this book, however, I have created a *Strategic Marketing Analysis* that focuses on the most important elements for a creative entrepreneur to consider without getting ridiculously weighed down in the minutiae of your creative business to the point where the process of planning becomes so overwhelming and dreadful that you don't even want to do it.

By making it user-friendly, I am hoping that it will not only help guide your business toward profitability, but also reinforce the value of strategic planning. As your business grows, I encourage you to read other business books that address the specific planning needs of larger businesses that are well established. No one book can ever cover every single eventuality that you will encounter in business so a well-read entrepreneur is more likely to be successful.

A strategic plan is usually intended for a business's internal use. It is a guide that the business can use as a road map toward growth. A business plan is usually intended for external use. For example, it could be shown to potential investors or a bank if you're trying to get a loan for your business.

How to Create a *Strategic Marketing Analysis*

As a solo creative entrepreneur, the traditional corporate marketing and business plan formats are cumbersome and most likely aren't really suitable for a lean operation such as yours. To make something useful for creative entrepreneurs, I tailored the essential components to the specific needs of artists, musicians, crafters, comedians, and other creative professionals.

STRATEGIC MARKETING ANALYSIS

Mission Statement
Here, you insert the mission statement you have created.

SWOT Analysis
(Strengths, Weaknesses, Opportunities, and Threats)
This section is very useful in giving you a coherent picture of your abilities and limitations. It is important to be as realistic as possible when you go through this exercise. I have found that people have a tendency to either be far too hard on themselves, as they assess their own abilities, or far too optimistic. If you're in doubt about your abilities, ask others for their assessment, particularly professionals in your field.

This part of the analysis covers important information because the strengths and weaknesses evaluate internal factors, while the opportunities and threats address external factors. Upon completing this section, you will have a much better idea of what you're dealing with and where you should focus your attention.

Strengths

This section examines the internal advantages of your business. Your personal resources, such as credentials, experience, and achievements can be listed here. Include your skills and abilities, while keeping in mind what differentiates you from your competition.

By knowing about your competitors, you can see where your skills and abilities fit into the marketplace. Do you do or offer something that they don't? Are you able to make yourself stand out by having your own schtick? Such important differentiating features can go a long way toward increasing your revenue. You may also discover a way in which you can charge less for your work than your competitors. If you're able to keep your overhead low, that should be a distinct advantage you have over competitors who may have top-heavy and inefficient organizations.

Weaknesses

This section examines the internal weaknesses of your business. Here, you can list any disadvantages you face, such as any lack of abilities, resources, or skills. By recognizing what needs to be strengthened, you can more effectively focus on what you can improve upon to build your business. For example, you may find that you need to take classes that will improve your skills or credentials. Or, you may need to work on obtaining funding for resources such as materials or storage space.

Opportunities

This section examines the external landscape in which you can attract more business. Here you can cite market trends that can help you gain an advantage in business that can drive your revenue. For example, if you're a clothing designer with a small boutique and your designs are in line with the latest fall fashions, that is a trend upon which you can capitalize to build your business.

Likewise, you may see obvious business opportunities in which you could cooperate with another business that serves the same target market you serve but isn't competing with you. By partnering with a non-competing business, you can expose your wares to new markets and get more mileage out of marketing efforts. The person with whom you partner will also be working to promote the joint venture so you essentially get twice the promotional benefit while doing only half the work.

As you look for opportunities that can advance your business, is there significant growth in a new technology that could help you reach more prospective customers? Things like new video technologies and developments in social media sites can be tremendously helpful in increasing your sales.

Threats

This section examines the external factors that threaten the health of your business. Threats could include things such as competitors' activities. For example, if one of your competitors has found a way to attract more business or charge less for their services, while still making a profit, such activity could have a dramatic effect on your business.

Another threat could be a new condition in the marketplace, such as a new law that forces you to pay an expensive tax or fee simply for doing business. For example, many entrepreneurs who created products for children, such as toys and jewelry, took a huge financial hit when the US government passed the Consumer Product Safety Improvement Act of 2008, which began requiring that these manufacturers submit their products for expensive lead testing that wasn't required before. While the law is obviously intended to protect children, a business owner in an affected industry needs to make significant changes to accommodate the new regulation.

Another example could be a threat from bad PR. If you're a musician and your genre of music is being criticized for being harmful to kids and teens, in the way that heavy metal and other genres were targeted by the Parents' Music Resource Center (PMRC) in the 1980s, even though you may not be recording songs with a negative message, you may suffer from being painted with the same broad brush as your fellow musicians.

GOST Analysis

(Goals, Objectives, Strategies, and Tactics)

Determining your goals, objectives, strategies, and tactics is critical because these are the mechanisms by which you can attain success. Here, you determine how exactly you will carry out the intentions of your mission statement.

Goals

Your goals broadly clarify exactly what you want to achieve and what form you want your business to take. The goals of an entrepreneur wishing to run and maintain a small family business will look very different from the goals of an entrepreneur who wants to grow a small business into an international corporation, even if the two businesses are producing the exact same products.

As you determine your goals, think in terms of a broad overview of the results you want to achieve. Your goals are high-level plans for your business. As such, they are not detailed in this section, but in others. A goal might look something like this:

- Grow market share in the tri-state area

- Hit the Billboard Hot 100

- Become the top-selling jewelry designer in the state

- Increase my comedy bookings this year

- Build brand equity in the wedding planning industry

Objectives

Your objectives state specifically how you plan to achieve your goals, essentially answering how you intend to get to where you want your business to be. Each objective should correlate directly to one of your listed goals. Your objectives should commit to specific and realistically achievable amounts and dates for completion of your activities. An objective of wanting to become a multi-million-dollar company a month after you've started your business would be extremely unrealistic, while an objective of doubling your sales figures from the first year to the second year may be perfectly reasonable and a solid objective.

It is critical that objectives are tied to specific numbers so you can actually measure your success. These numbers can be sales amounts, units sold, or other quantifiable measures. By citing specific quantities and financial amounts, you will have hard evidence of your accomplishments to better gauge how well your business is doing. This also empowers you to determine where you should focus more attention and which of your efforts have been most effective. Tracking numbers like sales amounts enables you to see how your actions increase or decrease sales so that you can modify your marketing efforts to earn more revenue.

As you determine your objectives, be sure not only to state what you'll do, but also when you'll do it. This will provide another way for you to make sure you're staying on track. As with all components of any marketing or business plan, the dates of completion should be realistic or you'll get discouraged.

When writing your objectives, be specific because vague objectives won't give you an effective way to measure your achievement. For example, "Advance my career" would be difficult to measure because it's so vague, but "Increase sales of my products by 30% in the second quarter" can be measured. An objective may look like this:

- Make 50% more in sales over the next six months

- Double my wedding bookings in May, June, and July of this year

- Reduce raw materials costs by 25% this year

- Upsell at least 75% of our existing customers' purchases in the fourth quarter

Over the years I have heard many marketers talk about *goals* and *objectives* as if they were synonymous and interchangeable. The definitions I present here, however, are widely recognized. While my fellow marketers continue to debate the definitions, the most important point I'm trying to make is that, basically, you should have a top level overview (in my example, the *goals*) and a more detailed look at how you will achieve these goals (in my example, the *objectives*). That being said, what you call them is far less important than actually *having* them, whatever you decide to call them.

In the corporate world, many marketers use two additional layers of detail when planning. These layers consist of *strategies* and *tactics*. For the purposes of this exercise, these are optional. If you were running a huge multinational corporation with millions of dollars at stake and resources being committed from various departments, then going into additional detail would be required. As a solo entrepreneur or the owner of a small business, it's far easier to keep track of who is doing what, when they're doing it, and why. If, however, you feel that going into this level of detail would help you, I have included descriptions and examples.

Strategies

Briefly stated, strategies establish the broad approach you will take to achieve your measurable objectives. As an example, if your objective was to *make 50% more in sales over the next six months*, your strategies to achieve that might include:

- Promote business through ads in local media

- Implement a social media campaign

- Offer discounts to increase sales

Tactics

Tactics provide the detail on which actions you will take to achieve your strategies. Your tactics may be similar to some of these:

- Send out press release on new gallery show

- Place quarter-page ads in XYZ Magazine

- Send 20% discount coupons to existing customer base

- Run banner ads on city's business website

- Send 500 direct mail brochures to prospective customers this month

Target Market

It is important to have a solid understanding of the people most likely to buy your products or services because, otherwise, you could end up wasting a tremendous amount of time and money aiming your marketing activities toward people who have absolutely no interest in what you're selling.

As you try to determine characteristics of your target market, be sure that what you're selling will fulfill the needs and/or desires of those customers. Think about which demographic groups your typical customer would fall into. An easy way to do this is to think about the people who enjoy your work the most. What are the most common characteristics of these people? Below are some questions about shared traits that can help you better identify your target market:

1) Is your work appreciated primarily by people in a certain area, such as the city versus rural areas?

2) Is one gender more interested in your work than the other? You may find that males and females are equally interested in your work.

3) While you may find people of all ages appreciating your work, what age group is most frequently represented?

4) What educational background do you see most commonly among people who enjoy your work?

5) What is the average income bracket that you see most commonly among people who enjoy your work?

6) Where do admirers of your work typically spend time? What websites do they frequent? What magazines and newspapers do they read? What TV shows do they watch? Where do they shop? What are their hobbies and interests?

These questions are by no means an exhaustive representation of what you can ask, but they're a good place to start. The better you understand the people who appreciate and are most likely to buy your products and services, the more effectively you can target your marketing to ensure they'll see and hear your messages. By knowing where people in your target market congregate, you'll know in which magazines and on what websites to advertise or try to get media coverage.

Once you have determined who is in your target market and know more about their behaviors and preferences, you will also be better able to determine the size of your market. If you sell something that appeals to a target market that is very large (e.g. suburban women, aged 25 - 54, with a college degree, earning $30,000 - $80,000), then you have much greater earning potential. That doesn't mean, however, that targeting a smaller niche market couldn't be profitable because it certainly can. It simply means that the creative entrepreneur targeting a smaller market may face more challenges. Whatever your target market and its size, however, embrace it and get to know the people within this market very well.

The Competitive Environment

Knowing what is going on within your business is of paramount importance, but it is also important to know what your competitors are doing. Everything they do affects the marketplace, which, in turn, affects your business.

Consider who else is selling to your target market. Some will be direct competitors, some won't. Those that sell essentially the same products or services to your target market are direct competitors.

Once you identify your competitors, examine the full range of what they are selling. Look at the types of promotions that they run. What are the similarities between your businesses and what are the differences? Should your business be doing similar promotions because of existing customer expectations, or should you be doing completely different promotions, which will draw attention to your business because of their novelty?

Every industry is different and promotions that worked five years ago may not work now so each businesses' situation needs to be analyzed independently. What is effective in one creative industry may not be effective in another.

It is valuable to have an idea of your market share. Market share is the proportion of the market that a given seller has. One artist may have 25% of the local market share while another has 4%. When you think of market share, imagine a pie chart that shows all of the competitors in a specific market. Each slice on that pie chart represents what proportion of total sales a particular seller has. Market share can be viewed for a local market, a national market, or an international market. While an artist who is very popular on the East Coast may have 38% of the regional market share in her market, the same artist may only have 1% of the national market share. Knowing how much market share you have versus your competitors gives you a better idea of your place in the market.

It can be extremely difficult for you to get a great deal of accurate sales information about your competitors. Whenever possible, however, base your measurements on hard numbers and accurate research. When you can't get exact numbers, at least try to approximate as realistically as possible.

Is your field crowded or open? The music industry represents an example of a very crowded field, while an art form using brand new computer technology that can be used to create innovative artwork may be so new that the field is very open because there are so few competitors.

How high are the barriers to entry in your field? The barriers to entry are the obstacles that make it more difficult for people to enter a particular market or field. These barriers are often economic. Fortunately, barriers can sometimes be lowered and even eliminated as new technologies are developed.

An example of this can be found in the publishing industry. Traditionally, writers had to rely on literary agents and book publishers to get their books printed and distributed to buyers. Those without professional connections or financial resources were at a distinct disadvantage. With the advent of print-on-demand (POD) technology, aspiring authors can now have their books available online within a few weeks, without having to jump through a book publisher's hoops or having to spend thousands of dollars to get their books printed. The traditional gatekeepers no longer have the ability to shut prospective authors out of the publishing industry because the barriers to entry have been lowered.

Another example is the music industry. Traditionally, aspiring musicians had to get through the music industry's gatekeepers such as A&R executives, DJs, and producers to even have a shot at getting a record deal. Because professional recording studios were prohibitively expensive and musicians didn't have an effective way to distribute their music on a large scale, they really needed the record labels. Since then, top-quality recording and mixing software has become very affordable and the Internet provides endless promotion and distribution options. Musicians no longer need the record companies in the same way, so the barriers to entry in the music business have also been significantly lowered.

Finances

As your business grows, it may be a good idea to hire a financial professional who can advise you how to keep the appropriate and necessary records for your business. I'm a marketer, not a financial professional, so I hire professionals who can guide me on the correct procedures and the latest laws.

Your financial needs can vary according to how your business is funded. If you are starting your business using money you have saved, and you find this to be sufficient to get started, your financial considerations will certainly be simpler than if you need to take out a loan or find investors.

By doing the exercises in this book, you will get a better idea of how much money you will need to start your business and on which resources you should spend those funds. Upon starting to sell, you should begin tracking how much money is coming in through sales versus how much money is going out in expenses.

An important factor to consider, as you develop your financial projections, is whether your business looks like it will make money. If your business costs are higher than the amount of money you can make in sales, your business won't be viable.

If your business grows significantly, it may reach the point at which you need to start creating financial documents, such as an income statement, a balance sheet, a cash-flow statement, a cash budget, and a break-even analysis. Since this book is intended to focus on small, creative businesses that are just beginning, such financial documents are outside the scope of this publication. However, there are a host of books on the market that can address these financial needs if or when they arise.

[NOTE: For the purpose of illustration, the following *Strategic Marketing Analysis* example uses fictional business scenarios for a fictional band. Any resemblance to actual business scenarios for an actual band are coincidental.]

Example of a *Strategic Marketing Analysis* for a Musician

To create your own strategic marketing analysis, simply go through the list of components detailed on the previous pages and fill in the information that pertains to your particular business. What follows is an example for a musician.

MUSICIAN'S *STRATEGIC MARKETING ANALYSIS*

Mission Statement

My mission is to become a full-time songwriter and musician providing recordings and live entertainment to an international audience.

SWOT Analysis

- **Strengths**
  - Staff to cover all major business functions
  - High-quality recording and production capabilities
  - Existing audience through platform on Internet radio show
  - Knowledgeable in guitar theory
  - Previous experience in public relations and sales
  - Good reputation on the local music scene
  - Have affordable office and rehearsal space
  - Differentiated from other bands in genre by a highly artistic retro sound and image

- **Weaknesses**
  - Insufficient funding to do a regional tour to promote new CD
  - Not well-known outside of local area
  - Need manager with connections to get into bigger venues
  - Inexperienced in arranging and managing an East Coast tour
  - Don't have enough video to use with online social media
  - Need money and resources to create videos

- **Opportunities**
  - Five new clubs have opened in the area
  - This genre is increasing in popularity
  - Huge national summer music festival coming to area and looking to book local acts
  - Local band just got signed, and we'd be a perfect fit as an opening act on tour

- **Threats**
  - Large local management firm has significant influence in getting its bands booked but isn't taking any new clients
  - Have large underage following that can't get into clubs
  - Facing competition from a band that is copying our sound and style
  - Some competing local bands have an "in" with a producer who has created a new, high-profile website that gives them national exposure

GOST Analysis

- **Goal**
  - Build the band's brand equity

- **Objective**
  - Increase club bookings by at least 75% for the next six

months

- **Strategy**
  - Promote the band to local booking agents

- **Tactics**
  - Send press kits to 25 local booking agents
  - Follow up mailing with calls to discuss booking opportunities

Target Market
International music fans aged 15 to 30 who like visually artistic bands with a retro sound, are heavy Internet users who actively seek new music, and live in households with incomes ranging from $50,000 to $120,000 per year.

The Competitive Environment
There are four direct competitors that we have identified in the tri-state area and 29 direct competitors nationally. The four regional competitors appear to have relatively the same resources as our band does, but five of the national competitors clearly have some sort of financial backing based on their high-end equipment, professionally designed websites, and superior music production.

Our market research, based solely on observable data, indicates that, locally, our band shares the market fairly evenly with our direct competitors. Each band holds approximately 20% of the regional market share based on local club performances and music sales. Nationally, our band appears to hold approximately 2% of the total market share in our specific genre of music.
Since this is a relatively new genre, and we are among the small number of bands driving the trend, we have an advantage over

any new bands about to enter the market because we already have an established fan base. Though we are primarily recognized regionally, we have had a couple of brief mentions in national music magazines that have columns highlighting various music trends across the country. We have also seen an increase in the number of fans willing to travel over 50 miles to see the band play.

As we work to gain more national market share, the primary barrier to entry has been a lack of finances. Because we don't have collateral for a loan, all of the band members are trying to work extra hours at our day jobs so we can save enough money to get a professional video made to increase our exposure on social media.

An advantage we have is that we have a larger repertoire of original songs than many competing bands. Additionally, we have better quality control of the music we offer to fans online. Many of our competitors offer a few well-recorded songs, with the rest sounding like very rough demos.

We have recently started working with a county charity that supports keeping music in our local schools. We have played two benefit gigs so far to help raise money for the charity. They advertise in all of the local papers and on the radio, which has given us a great deal of media coverage.

Finances

Up until now, we have been funding the band's activities with personal money we have saved from our day jobs and money we make from our gigs after we have paid the sound engineer and lighting tech. While this has been enough to help us get the equipment and other resources we have needed to reach our current status, we just aren't bringing in enough money with our current gig schedule to have a professional video made. In response, we have calculated that, if we book five additional gigs per month, in three months we will have enough to have a video made by a local firm we have chosen.

We are making enough money on music and merchandise sales to pay for more recording, CD manufacturing, and t-shirts. Up until now, we have had to buy CDs and t-shirts in smaller quantities, but our sales are increasing significantly so we are quickly approaching a point at which we can order in greater volume. At that point, our per-unit costs will drop, and we will make more money per item sold. This additional revenue will help contribute to new marketing activities.

CHAPTER 18

How to Choose a Business Model

Different Kinds of Business Models

Over my years of working with creative entrepreneurs, they have frequently told me that one of the biggest challenges they face is trying to come up with a **business model** that will work for them. Once you have completed your ***Analysis of Resources*** and your ***Strategic Marketing Analysis***, you are very well positioned to select a business model that can generate income for you.

Any business model you choose must be clear and achievable. Now that you have gone through the process of looking at your resources and the overall marketplace, you know what you have to work with and what you need. Keeping these factors in mind will help you select the business model that's right for you.

What is a business model? While there are plenty of rather convoluted definitions out there, simply put, a business model is the structure that a business uses to make money. You are already familiar with many different business models, whether you realize it or not.

A vegetable farmer has a business model in which he or she grows and sells produce. This is a very traditional and simple business model. It can be very direct, in that the farmer can sell directly to consumers, or the farmer can be part of a larger business chain in which he or she may sell to companies that use the produce in other products, such as vegetable soup. In the second scenario, the farmer isn't dealing directly with the consumers who will ultimately eat the soup. The farmer is making money from the soup manufacturer.

Another very common business model is an advertisement model. In this model, a business offers free content to an audience to attract as many people as possible and, then, earns its money by selling advertisements. This can be found on most basic television channels, some free print publications, and many websites. The more viewers, readers, or visitors the business can bring in, the more the business can charge for its ads. This is why ads broadcast during major sporting events cost so much. Since the biggest events have such vast audiences, a hefty price can be commanded for the commercial time because so many people will see the ads that run during those games.

In contrast, a subscription model charges a fee for access to content or services. This is the model used by premium cable channels, many educational business programs that offer exclusive content to entrepreneurs, and some websites that cater to a small niche of business professionals. If your business caters to a smaller and more specialized audience, you may not have enough people to enable you to charge a lot for advertising so subscription fees may be a better option for you.

High-end fashion magazines use both advertising and subscriptions to cover their expenses and make money. Their glossy, full-color pages don't come cheap so they sell many ads, while still charging readers a premium price per issue.

You could use a business model in which you create your own website and sell directly to customers. A challenge in using this type of model is in how you will let people know about your business. Without regular web traffic, sales will undoubtedly suffer. Advertising to let people know about your business is expensive so you could incur significant advertising expenses using this model.

Selling on websites that already have regular traffic and many buyers who are interested and ready to make a purchase could be an alternative model. By selling on sites like Etsy.com, Upillar.com, and eBay, you can move merchandise more quickly and won't incur the expenses of having a retail website created for your business and buying advertising to bring Web traffic to your site.

Your choice of business model will also be affected depending on whether you're selling directly to businesses (**business-to-business** or **B2B**) or directly to consumers (**business-to-consumer** or **B2C**). It is wise to select a business model that your prospective customers find comfortable and easy to use.

There are certainly additional business models, but those already mentioned are among the most common you'll encounter. As with many aspects of business, there isn't always a "right" or "wrong" option. What works best for your needs and the needs of your customers is right for your business.

Why Clarity Is Important

Your business model must be clear. If your model is nebulous, it will be ineffective in bringing in revenue. There is no room for a lack of focus in determining a business model. For example, if you create a content-driven website, will you make money from advertising or by selling membership-only access to the website content? There is a huge difference between these two models.

In this example, if you select an advertising model, then you want to drive as much traffic as possible to your website because the more unique visitors you have, the more you can charge for ads. Will your content change frequently enough to encourage visitors to come back often and tell others about your website? Will you sell ads yourself or hire a sales team? What kinds of companies will you target for ad sales?

If you decide to use a subscription model, how many visitors do you think you can convert to subscribers? Can you sell enough subscriptions to make the amount of revenue you need and want? How much will you charge for subscriptions? Is your content strong enough and unique enough to draw in subscribers, or can they get similar information on websites that don't require subscriptions?

As you can see in these two cases, the business model you choose will have a tremendous impact on how you earn money and run your business. There are many aspects that should be considered and studied carefully. Every business is different, as are the needs of owners and customers. It is important that your business model fits your particular business well so it runs smoothly and efficiently and so that you can bring in the amount of revenue you want.

CHAPTER 19

Effective Marketing Planning

Planning Your Marketing

Once you understand exactly what you want to do professionally, what resources you have, what resources you need, and what kind of business model will work the best for your business, then you'll need to begin planning how to get where you want to be. Your strategy needs to be clear, targeted, measurable, and realistic, in order to work. While business can be filled with unexpected twists and turns at the best of times, it is very important to plan the specific steps you want to take to achieve your business goals, to avoid as many surprises as possible.

Saying, "I want to sell lots of products," is a vague goal that doesn't provide any direction. Instead, it would be better to set a goal such as, "I want to reach an audience of 100,000 prospects interested in my products and convert 5% of them to customers." That is measurable, which will help you determine whether you have been successful, after you take that step.

If you are successful, you are most likely on the right track. If not, ask yourself why. Are you incorrectly defining your target market? If you're still not clear about who is in your target market, review chapter 11 in this book again and see if, perhaps, there is another angle you may not have considered before. Accurately recognizing your target market is critical to your success.

As you develop the specifics of your marketing plans, it is important to think about your marketing mix. The marketing mix consists of the following:

PRODUCT
PRICE
PLACE (DISTRIBUTION)
PROMOTION

All of these components are critically important to the success of your business. I will address each of these in more detail.

Product

First, you need to determine *what* you will be selling. Will you sell tangible products, services, or both?

Next, determine your position in the market. How will you be branding yourself? Are you in a high-end market, an inexpensive market, or somewhere in between? Are you offering something at a low price for mass consumption or are you selling something at a high price that will sell fewer units? Your pricing will affect how you present your wares to the world. Some of this is out of necessity, simply because a lower price range will not readily accommodate expensive ad campaigns and expensive marketing materials. For example, if you are selling an item at $7.00 per unit, paying $4.00 per unit for glossy, four-color marketing folders and brochures would be prohibitively expensive. But, if you are selling something that costs $100,000 per unit, suddenly, spending $4.00 on marketing materials to convert a prospect into a customer isn't unreasonable.

At what level of quality are you selling? There can be value for customers at all price points so tremendously expensive products and services aren't necessarily better for either your business or your revenue potential. If you can sell a product or service at a low price for a segment of the market that needs something in a lower price range, you may be able to sell so much that you can earn very impressive revenue.

How will you package and present your product or service? Your packaging and marketing materials should reflect the price point and customer expectations of your product or service.

Price

Determining pricing is a challenge for any entrepreneur but, perhaps, even more so for creative entrepreneurs who need to build more soft costs, such as their own time spent working, into the final price of a product or service. How, for example, does a jewelry designer determine what price to charge for beaded necklaces? Let's say the cost of the materials to make a necklace is $10. If it takes two hours to make one necklace, how much should the designer charge for that time spent actually making the piece?

Let's look at it this way: If the designer works eight hours a day, and each necklace takes two hours to make, then four necklaces can be produced per day. How much money does the designer need to make to stay in business? If the designer needs to make $180 a day (don't forget to factor taxes into your prices, when you calculate this for yourself), then the cost of the designer's time per necklace needs to be $45 because $180 per day ÷ 8 hours = $22.50 per hour (or $45 for the two hours spent to make each necklace). Then, the cost of materials ($10) needs to be added in so the price per necklace increases to $55 because **$45 time cost + $10 materials cost = $55 per necklace**.

The next consideration for the designer is to find out if there are customers willing to pay $55 per necklace. Are other designers selling similar necklaces for a higher or a lower price? If they are selling similar products for less, perhaps the designer can do something to differentiate the necklaces and make them warrant a higher price. If that is not an option, the only other direction the designer can go in is to find effective ways to reduce the price without reducing the amount of income.

> **If you build strong brand equity, you may find that you can actually charge *more* than your competitors.**

In this case, the designer either needs to obtain materials at a lower cost or to increase efficiency so that necklaces can be made in less time. In such a case, if the designer can get materials for each necklace at a cost of $5, that can reduce the cost of the necklace to $50 per necklace, without affecting the amount of income the designer is making. If, however, competitors are selling similar products at $40 per necklace, the designer can still lose business to competitors.

If the designer can find a more efficient way to produce the necklaces, then more can be made in the same span of an eight-hour day, and the designer can maintain the same amount of income. If there is a way to make each necklace in one hour, the equation then looks like this: **$22.50 time cost + $5 materials cost = $27.50 per necklace**. Additionally, since necklaces can now be made in one hour instead of two, the designer can produce eight necklaces per day. This means that, for one day's work, the potential for income is still $180 because eight necklaces at a time cost of $22.50 per hour is $180. The income has remained the same, yet the price per unit has decreased, thus making the designer's products more appealing to consumers than competitors' products.

Keep in mind that brand equity can completely change this scenario. If you build strong brand equity, you may find that you can actually charge *more* than your competitors, despite the cost of materials, and still earn higher revenues than your competition. Think about the market for designer handbags. Let's be honest, these aren't made of gold, they're made of the same types of materials as other handbags. Sure, the materials are generally better quality, but the cost of those higher quality materials still doesn't warrant prices in the thousands. Generally, these types of companies do spend a great deal of money on advertising in high-profile fashion magazines featuring glossy ads by top photographers and graphic designers but, even factoring in those costs, a handbag needn't cost thousands of dollars. Why do customers pay those prices? Mainly because they want to project a certain image.

Let's say the necklace designer mentioned earlier decides to use this type of strategy. It will be expensive to build upmarket brand equity but, if the sales support the strategy, it could work. The trade-off is that the designer will sell less product but make a higher profit on each piece. This reinforces the exclusivity felt by customers who don't want to see their jewelry style being worn by everyone else.

Another consideration to keep in mind, when determining price, is how the transaction looks from the customer's perspective. While sellers would like to have the luxury of *telling* the market what the value of products and services should be, it is actually customers who determine the value. As consumers examine their various options in the marketplace, they consider the balance of factors, such as quality, price, convenience, durability, performance, maintenance costs, and prestige. *Price* is not synonymous with *value*. Instead, price is a component in the equation that determines value. It can be looked at this way:

Value = Benefits - Price

If a customer feels that the benefits gained from a product or service outweigh the price that was paid, then the customer feels that he or she received value. When the price outweighs the benefits, however, there is no value to a customer.

The least expensive option isn't always the one that offers the best value. Charging higher prices won't necessarily cause you to lose business, if you can deliver what your customers want.

Place (Distribution)

If you're selling physical products, how will you get them to buyers? The pipeline you use to get your products to consumers is known as a **distribution channel**. This could be as simple as selling directly to consumers through your own website or store or, depending on what you're selling and the needs of your business, your distribution channel may be longer because it has one or more **intermediaries** (or **middlemen**) between you and the consumers who will ultimately use your products. The intermediaries you will most likely encounter as a creative entrepreneur are **distributors**, **wholesalers**, and **retailers**. Distributors and wholesalers would, typically, buy from you then sell to retailers. Retailers would then, typically, sell to consumers. If your distribution channel involves intermediaries other than those I have mentioned, you are probably working at a more complex level and will be dealing with business transactions that are outside the scope of this book.

As you consider whether you want to sell directly to customers or through a longer distribution channel, keep in mind that each intermediary in the channel will need to make money in the process. The more intermediaries in the channel, the higher the price of your product by the time it reaches consumers.

If you're selling physical products, how will you get them to buyers?

While it may be tempting to sell direct so you don't have to pay a middleman, many intermediaries offer a great deal of value and can increase your quantity of sales, thereby increasing your total revenue. They may have established relationships with retailers that would otherwise be difficult to access. They may also handle many business transactions that will free you up to focus more on the production of your product than the distribution of it. When selecting a distributor, look for one that is a good fit for your particular business. Pay close attention to logistical factors, such as warehousing, transportation, and order fulfillment.

If you decide to sell direct and also sell through retailers, be aware that selling at a lower price than retailers gives them no reason to offer your products to their customers, since your lower prices will cause consumers to buy directly from you. Having your products available through retailers is valuable in that it increases your products' exposure to consumers and creates more points of contact with prospective buyers. The more consumers see your products, the more likely they are to buy because the opportunity is presented more frequently.

Promotion

How will you let consumers know about what you are selling? Simply making products or services available won't drive sales. It is important to let consumers know that your products and services are available, since people can't buy something if they don't even know it exists in the first place. Be sure to communicate value to buyers and give them a compelling reason to purchase from you rather than your competitors.

Simply making products or services available won't drive sales.

You may eventually have a sales force to handle **personal selling**, which is done on an individual basis when a salesperson sells to and builds relationships with customers. It is still important, however, to design an advertising and PR campaign so you can reach large numbers of people with messages about what you are selling.

There are various places to promote your business, such as magazines, websites, newspapers, radio, and television. To get into any of these, you can either buy ads or try to get free media coverage. Advertising and publicity are covered in greater detail in chapters 24 and 25.

Another important component of promotion is your presentation. A common mistake people make is to try to cram far too much information into any presentation of their products or services. Different types of presentation include websites, product packaging, marketing materials, press releases, and ads. The goal of presentation is to give an appropriate amount of information for the particular objective.

For example, the primary function of your website is to inform and sell. If the site is difficult to navigate or too weighed down with text, visitors probably won't get the message you want them to receive. Make sure that the navigation on your website is intuitive so customers can easily find what they're searching for. If people have to spend too much time looking for products or information, they'll be less likely to come back.

The novelty of technical bells and whistles wears off quickly and, if these elements slow down a user's experience because the files are big and slow to load, customers soon grow tired of them. Generally, a nice, clean, and organized site is the best way to go.

Frequently in marketing, less is more. By simply paring down the copy on your website, your message may become *more* effective instead of *less* effective. Clear, concise information is much easier for people to process than cluttered information, yet I can't tell you how many times clients have insisted on filling every bit of space on a website, only to later wonder why they didn't get responses.

When designing product packaging, take a look at what the most professional companies do. Typically, their packaging is easy to read, streamlined, and provides the information that is required, without being overwhelming. It should look appealing to customers and will often contain clues about what a customer can expect from the product. For example, diet products often have a lot of green on their packaging so they look fresh and natural. High-end products are more likely to have metallic ink on their packaging. Cheaper products are more likely to feature fluorescent colors and contain intentional misspellings of words, such as “valu” instead of “value,” in the product name.

The objective of marketing materials is to let a potential customer know why your product or service is preferable to others available in the marketplace. These materials represent your business so they should accurately reflect what you’re selling. In my experience, bullet points get better results than big blocks of dense text. I have measured response rates in many marketing campaigns, and marketing copy presented in the form of bullet points has always performed better. I believe it’s simply because it is easier for readers to process.

Additionally, keep in mind that people are very busy. If a marketing piece has a large amount of text describing an offer, people often feel overwhelmed and decide to put the materials aside and read them later when they have more time. Unfortunately, there are so many things competing for the attention of consumers that they rarely get around to reading the materials later.

Another factor to bear in mind, as you create marketing materials, is to keep them simple. The more bits and pieces that are involved, the less likely that prospects will read and save them. For example, rather than having an intricate marketing piece that folds out in ten different directions and has small sticky notes attached, make the materials streamlined. What are prospects more likely to read, a concisely-worded marketing brochure or a marketing piece that is the size of a small book?

CHAPTER 20

Making the Sale

Marketing Communication That Delivers Results

What makes a customer decide to buy from a particular seller? Certainly, an appealing product or service that offers value is a large part of the equation, but communication also plays a huge role.

When communicating sales information to customers, less is definitely more. Over the years, I have tested response rates on marketing pieces in a variety of industries and, every time, I found a direct correlation between the length of the copy and the response rate. The more concise the copy, the higher the response rate. A strong and brief offering is easier for a busy person to mentally process, and he or she can quickly make a decision whether or not to buy.

The more concise the copy, the higher the response rate.

Another important consideration, when you write marketing copy to sell your products or services, is to factor in the reader's question of, "What's in it for me?" What value can you communicate to people that will cause them to feel that, by missing out on your offering, they'll be missing out on something that can help them save money or time, enjoy quality entertainment, live a better life, find the happiness that eludes them, etc.?

Don’t Let the First Sale Be the Last Sale

It’s always important to get new sales but, as you work on a long-term strategy for your business, it’s important to keep customers coming back. Driving repeat sales is one of the most effective ways to increase revenue.

Acquiring new customers costs your business more because you bear the expense of attracting them. This expense is made up of advertising costs, marketing costs, PR, Internet promotion, your time, branded promotional items, mailing costs, etc. Getting new customers takes a great deal of work and, as an entrepreneur, you may have to do all of the work yourself, which takes time away from other things you want to do to build your business.

Once you’ve done all the hard work of getting a customer to buy from you for the first time, the cost of retaining that customer is significantly lower. The customer now recognizes your brand, has tried your product or service, and has been pleased. Once someone recognizes the value your business offers, that person is much more likely to buy again.

The next step in building your customer base is to retain existing customers and sell to them again. Below are a number of easy ways to do this:

Offer products at various price points.

Prospects will be more likely to purchase a less expensive product or service from you, as a way to try out what you have to offer. They want to test out the quality and effectiveness. By offering products and services at low, medium, and high price points, you give customers the opportunity to make purchases at their various comfort levels and within their own budgets, at any given time. What you will most likely see is customers entering at a lower price point, then increasing their purchase amounts with subsequent purchases.

Stay in front of customers with free offers.

Offer value to your customers with free ezines, free webinars, or free telephone conferences. This is not only an effective way to familiarize prospects and new customers with your business, but it also gives them a reason to maintain a line of communication with you. Likewise, it provides you with repeated marketing opportunities, while it strengthens your brand.

Create a simple referral program.

Often your best advocates are existing customers. By offering some sort of reward for referrals, you can encourage customers who genuinely value your business to tell others about it. Make sure that any referral program you design is easily trackable so that neither you nor your customers are burdened with tracking results. Using something simple, like unique discount codes that new customers can use when placing orders, can be a very effective way to track success and reward customers who referred business to you. Additionally, it will prevent these codes from being used on discount code listing websites, which would not only defeat the purpose of your program, but also reduce your revenue in a way that you can't anticipate or effectively build into your marketing costs.

Feature customer testimonials.

As you get positive feedback from customers, put it where other prospects and customers will see it. After getting written permission, you can feature it on your website and marketing materials. The type of customer feedback that will be most likely to influence prospects to buy cites specific aspects of a product or service, such as durability, value, cost-effectiveness, or quality. Prospects are very interested to know what kind of positive results they can expect, if they buy from you.

Sell more at checkout.

One of the best times to sell is at the point of purchase. This is why grocery stores offer items by the register while customers are waiting their turn to pay for their purchases. At this stage of the purchasing process, customers are very likely to make impulse buys. Frequently, offering an additional, inexpensive item or a small discount on a more expensive item can encourage customers to buy more from you.

Promote holiday specials.

The holidays can be a great time to bundle products and services for sale or to offer things that you don't offer during the rest of the year. Businesses from spas to microbreweries use these strategies very effectively.

Offer volume discounts.

A great way to increase sales volume is to offer discounts when customers purchase more. Selling larger quantities to a few customers is more cost effective than selling smaller amounts to a greater number of customers. Volume discounts provide great value to both you and your customers.

Will Social Media Increase Your Sales?

The frenzy over how to use social media as a marketing tool reminds me of the heady days of the dot-com gold rush in the nineties. With everyone in business looking for the latest and greatest ways to increase sales, can social media applications really deliver on the fulfillment of such lofty business expectations?

Here are a few considerations to help you determine how large a role social media should play in your overall marketing strategy:

How much time are you spending on social networking sites?

While these sites provide yet another opportunity to post a virtual billboard on the information superhighway, they need to be maintained with fresh content, which can take a considerable amount of time that could be spent on other sales activities.

Are your social networking efforts increasing your sales?

Is the time spent maintaining these sites commensurate with the sales they drive to your business? Are you even able to measure how much business is driven by these activities? Branding activities can be very worthwhile, but it's important to implement some sort of mechanism that enables you to track where customers are coming from so you know where to focus your efforts.

It is up to each entrepreneur to determine the balance between time spent on social media and the sales these efforts affect. Social media can be more effective for some businesses than others, depending on what you're selling, and should be used in coordination with other marketing tools, not as the sole method of marketing.

Are you capturing visitor contact information for future marketing activities?

People who visit your social networking sites have some level of interest in what you do. They also have busy lives and get distracted. It's important to have some way of getting in touch with them in the future so you can let them know about your new business offerings.

People who have already visited your sites online are some of the best leads you can get. Having them follow you on social networking sites is good, but getting their email addresses for future marketing is even better. Direct contact information from qualified leads is marketing gold.

Are social networking sites driving traffic to your website?

With the tremendous number of demands on people's attention, their interests can quickly move onto other things. Consider the mass migration of people from MySpace to Facebook. Next, Twitter became the hot form of social media, but there will undoubtedly be other sites coming in the future that will attract users away from the forms they currently use. It is valuable to have sites on social media where people can discover you, but be sure to convert them to regular visitors to your website as the primary hub for information about your business.

Be ready for change.

As new forms of social media are added to the already long list of Internet offerings, be ready to go where the action is.

CHAPTER 21

Selling Your Wares

The Difference Between a Hobby and a Business

It is easy to see the distinction between a hobby and a business. When someone wants to work on an artistic pursuit and maintain complete artistic integrity with no influence whatsoever from sales figures, they can have a very satisfying hobby. There is nothing at all wrong with doing that. Having a hobby means that you never have to please anyone but yourself. You may even sell some products and services but, as long as it's only a hobby, there is no pressure to increase sales because it is done for your personal enjoyment.

Once a creative person decides to turn their hobby into a business, the very nature of this endeavor is different from a hobby because, as a business, profitability becomes important. Additionally, what prospects and customers think and want is suddenly of paramount importance. There is nothing wrong with this, either, and it doesn't necessarily mean you have to compromise your artistic integrity. Some artists feel that their artistic vision is threatened if they start a business. Creating a business doesn't mean an artist or creative person has to "sell out" to the market, but it does require a perspective that is different from what one has when engaging in a hobby.

For example, if an artist is creating a product that only appeals to a very small niche audience, the price per unit will need to be higher because the artist will sell fewer units. If an artist is willing to create additional products that appeal to a broader audience, that person can sell for a lower per-unit cost because more products can be sold.

To look at an actual example, let's say we know two artists who make metal sculpture. One of these artists, Kate, has very eccentric tastes that appeal to a small number of prospective customers. Another artist, Deborah, enjoys creating avant-garde pieces but is also willing to make some pieces that appeal to more traditional types of buyers. In order for each artist to make $40,000 in sales a year, how much will each one need to charge per piece? If Deborah can sell each piece for $400, plus her materials costs, she needs to sell 100 pieces during the course of a year to earn $40,000. If her work has a broader appeal, she may very well sell even more than that. As she becomes more popular and well known, she will also be able to more easily increase her prices.

With Kate's more narrow appeal, however, she may only be able to sell 25 sculptures in a year. To make $40,000 in sales for the year, she'd need to charge $1,600 per piece, plus her materials costs. The question is, will Kate's customers value her work enough to pay that amount? While she only needs 25 people to reach the desired annual sales, can she find at least that many people willing to pay that amount for one of her eccentric sculptures?

If Kate is very focused on her target market and knows where and how to appeal to them, she may very well be able to reach this sales goal, while still creating art that is exactly what she wants to create and without modifying anything to try to increase sales. Additionally, if she can build strong brand equity, she will even be able to charge higher prices. If she is unable to build brand equity, however, she may find herself out of business very quickly and working in an office job that she hates, while Deborah is living as a full-time working artist.

A more realistic route to success is to at least begin by appealing to a broader audience of consumers. Once you have established yourself a bit, then it's easier to pick and choose what kind of work you want to do.

If you decide to start a business, it's important to sell what people are willing to buy, rather than only selling something you like regardless of whether or not anyone else likes it. I am continually amazed by the role that ego can play in destroying businesses, when I see shows like *Ramsay's Kitchen Nightmares*. In addition to the customer service issues the show highlights, mentioned in chapter 12, the program illustrates why sellers have difficulty selling. Over and over, the same scenario is played out as a stubborn business owner insists on selling what he or she wants to sell instead of what customers want to buy. Despite consultation from Gordon Ramsay, one of the few chefs in the world to maintain a three-star Michelin ranking, the struggling restaurant owner would seemingly rather go bankrupt than sell what customers want to buy. It sounds like a simple concept to understand yet, every year, countless business owners lose money for this very same reason. As a business owner, you can certainly love what you sell, but maintaining enough professional distance and objectivity to make sound business decisions is critical to your success.

Different Types of Product Offerings

To go from a hobby to a business by focusing on making a profit, you'll first need something to sell. If you create tangible products, such as clothing, paintings, photographs, sculptures, jewelry, handbags, printed t-shirts, floral wreaths, ornaments, etc., you can sell items you have already created, sell custom-made items, or sell both types of products. If you sell a service, such as performing music, comedy, or dance, you deliver the "product" as you are performing it for an audience. Certainly, you can sell both, just as a musician can sell a service while performing music, then also sell tangible products, such as music downloads, t-shirts, and programs.

There are very distinct pros and cons to each type of selling. Below are some to consider, before you commit extensive time and resources to your endeavor. By evaluating your options in advance, you can make the decisions that will be best for you and your business.

Selling Premade Tangible Items

PROS: Because you make these items in advance, you have the advantage of easily being able to show potential customers exactly what they can buy. Customers can immediately determine whether they like the items you have for sale.

CONS: Unless you produce a significant variety of items in advance, the selection you offer to potential customers will be narrow. This can result in fewer sales because a limited variety of products will appeal to a smaller number of consumers. The challenge, however, in creating a wider range of items is that you bear the cost burdens up front. This includes not only the costs of materials, but also the cost of your time to make these items. You will spend money before you make any money.

Selling Custom-Made Items

PROS: An advantage to this type of selling is that you have lower, if any, up-front costs because you don't make a product until a customer orders one.

CONS: A disadvantage is the high potential for a customer to refuse to pay for a custom item because you didn't create it exactly the way the customer envisioned the finished product. You should request a deposit before starting work so that you have funds to pay for the materials and to partially protect yourself against the risk of customers simply not paying. (Be sure to get customer approval during the progression of the item, to ensure customer satisfaction and final payment for the completed item.)

Selling a Service

PROS: An advantage to this type of selling is that you have lower, if any, up-front costs.

CONS: A disadvantage to this type of selling is that you don't have a tangible product to sell. Instead, you need to represent your service through various means, such as marketing brochures, press releases, press coverage, video clips, audio clips, etc. (These marketing pieces will show prospects what you can do for the money you are charging. They will help prospects with their purchasing decisions.)

CHAPTER 22

Tracking Your Success

Ways to Track Performance

The longer you're in business, the more sales data you will accrue. This information provides you with a valuable mechanism with which to measure your success. Tracking and analyzing your sales are key to becoming more successful. Using historical sales data can help you increase your current sales; you can more easily see trends so you can determine what's working and what needs to be improved.

Of course, if you're just starting out, you won't have any previous sales information to analyze. As you accumulate data, you will be able to use it to help in making wise business decisions.

While this can seem quite tedious, the information you get from looking at historical sales data can be invaluable. By getting into the habit of analyzing your sales each month, you can react more quickly to keep your sales on course. This is much better than waiting six months or a year to analyze all of your accumulated sales data. After that much time has gone by, you may have missed significant selling opportunities.

Marketers have formulas to measure various aspects of a business looking forward, backward, and sideways. Instead of overwhelming you with marketing formulas, I have included some that I think will be most useful to you as you get started.

[NOTE: For the sake of clarity, I have addressed most of these in terms of how they would be used to measure website sales, but they can also be used to measure off-line sales.]

Average Order Value (AOV)

Measuring the average amount a customer spends on your website is helpful for a number of reasons. Let's say you have a website on which you sell a variety of crafts that you have made. If you're selling a wide range of products, such as scented candles, holiday wreaths, and beaded jewelry, it's important to know how much the average buyer purchases on your site.

Are people visiting your website looking for one particular item, then finding additional products that they like enough to purchase? This is important to measure because you want to know if your website is effectively promoting additional products to visitors so you can increase your sales. Someone might visit your site just looking for a candle and end up buying not only that, but several other items that also looked appealing.

It is wise to examine the AOV to get a better understanding of the purchasing behavior of various segments of your customer base. For example, you would want to know if the AOV of first-time customers is high, then drops significantly for subsequent purchases. If that is the case, being aware of that trend can help you find ways to increase the AOV of repeat customers.

This measurement can also point out the most profitable sources of website traffic. This is tremendously helpful as you work to improve your advertising strategy. An examination of your AOV may show you that new customers who used an online discount code you placed in a local magazine ad had a higher AOV than customers who used a different discount code you placed on a website ad. This information shows you where your most profitable customers are coming from, which can enable you to make wiser decisions about where you want to spend your advertising budget.

You can determine the AOV using the following formula:

$$\textbf{(total sales)} \div \textbf{(\# orders)} = \textbf{AOV}$$

This could be applied to the sales data below as follows:

Month	Total Sales	Total Orders	AOV
Jan.	$1320	88	$15
Feb.	$1786	94	$19
Mar.	$1818	101	$18
April	$1800	100	$18
May	$1881	99	$19
June	$6820	124	$55
July	$6678	126	$53
Aug.	$2040	102	$20
Sept.	$1805	95	$19
Oct.	$3216	134	$24
Nov.	$3996	148	$27
Dec.	$5024	157	$32

I've kept the numbers simple so they're easy to follow. As you can see in the example, the AOV increased slightly during the last three months of the year, as did the total number of orders. This is not unusual and can, most likely, be attributed to holiday sales. What really stands out, however, is the jump in AOV that occurred during June and July. Seeing such a dramatic difference in your sales numbers alerts you to investigate why there was such a sharp increase for those two months. If you can determine what caused the increase in the AOV, you can try to capitalize on whatever boosted those sales. You would want to see if there was a big event occurring over the summer that caused people to purchase more of your products. Did you run a particularly effective sale by offering customers a percentage off, which drove them to buy more?

The more thoroughly you can understand why your sales increase and decrease, the better positioned you are to take steps to control and increase your sales. Pay close attention to customer behavior so you learn what your customers want.

Conversion Rate

The conversion rate is an important measure because it tells you how many of your website visitors have become customers.

To calculate your online conversion rate:

(# orders) ÷ (# clicks) = conversion rate

So, if you have 120 orders and 3000 clicks, your rate is 4%.

If you're doing a direct mail promotion in which you're sending marketing information to targeted prospects to drive your sales, you can also use this formula. For example, if your direct mail piece has a postcard for prospects to send back to you to get something such as more information, a free trial, or a discount coupon, measuring the conversion rate will show you the effectiveness of your direct mail campaign.

To calculate the conversion rate of a direct mail campaign:

(# orders) ÷ (# responses) = conversion rate

People often ask what is considered a good conversion rate, but it can vary so widely depending on your particular business that there isn't really one number by which to judge it. It's more important to work to improve your own conversion rate, whatever that may be. As you continue to measure various sales performance numbers for your own business, you will be accumulating historical data so that, eventually, you can compare this year's sales to last year's sales and, later, to the sales over the course of several years. Your historical sales data is a gold mine of useful information with which you can build your business.

Once you have at least a year's worth of sales data for your business, you will be able to more accurately predict what sales will be because you have trends to which you can refer. Obviously, the more data you have, the more accurately you can predict your sales figures. This enables you to decide whether you'd like to run a specific promotional campaign again. Using the direct mail example, if you have run a few direct mail campaigns and your average conversion rate has been 2%, you can use that information to determine whether it's cost effective to run another similar promotion.

To calculate how many orders you can expect based on your average conversion rate:

(avg. conversion rate) x (# responses) = (expected # of orders)

So, if your average conversion rate is 2%, and you typically get 150 responses, then you could reasonably expect to get 3 orders from this promotion. Will the money you make from those 3 sales be sufficient to cover the expenses of doing this promotion? If you have a high profit margin, it may be worth spending the money on this promotion but, if you don't, you may want to consider different ways to increase sales.

Click-Through Rate (CTR)

The click-through rate tells you how successful an online advertising campaign has been by measuring the percentage of people who clicked on an online ad.

To calculate the click-through rate for an online ad:

(# of clicks on the ad) ÷ (# of impressions) = CTR

The number of impressions indicates the number of times that ad appeared online so, if your online ad was clicked 25 times and it had 1,000 impressions, then your CTR would be 2.5%.

As with trying to determine good conversion rates, there are so many variables that finding a good average CTR across industries, even within industries, is nearly impossible. Again, it is best to track the historical data for your own business and use that performance information as the standard upon which you'll work to improve.

Measuring Online Ad Performance

Since some of the most affordable and most effectively targeted ads you can buy are online, simply knowing how to determine the conversion rate and the CTR can be tremendously helpful as you measure the performance of any online ads you purchase. By tracking the performance of your online ads, you can see where your hard-earned money is most effectively spent.

Below is an example of a simple tracking sheet you could easily set up using a computer spreadsheet program.

Online Ads	**Impressions**	**Clicks**	**CTR**	**Orders**	**Conversion**
Local Website	10,000	100	1.0%	3	3.0%
City Website	50,000	200	0.4%	1	0.5%
National Website	150,000	1,200	0.8%	19	1.6%

In the example above, we can see that the local website and the national website have better CTRs than the city website. The local and national sites also show better conversion rates. To determine if it is worth the price to continue advertising on these sites, however, we need to look at additional data. We need to examine the amount of **profit** that came in through this particular online ad campaign. The profit is determined by taking the amount you made in sales and subtracting the costs to make the products.

Online Ads	Orders	Total Profit
Local Website	3	$475.00
City Website	1	$130.00
National Website	19	$2,900.00

Based on the profit totals, it could be easy to come to the conclusion that the national website is the best place to advertise, but we still have to consider how much it costs to advertise there. If we are spending more money to advertise than we are bringing in from sales, the ads aren't cost effective.

Online Ads	Total Profit	Ad Cost per Impression	Impressions	Total Ad Cost
Local Website	$475.00	$0.005	10,000	$50.00
City Website	$130.00	$0.01	50,000	$500.00
National Website	$2,900.00	$0.01	150,000	$1,500.00

As you can see, when you look at the profit amounts compared to what was spent in advertising, the picture becomes clearer. The local website delivered more in profit than what the ad cost, but the city website cost more than the amount of profit it delivered. The national website is expensive, but was profitable.

If you're buying ads for the first time and don't have a big advertising budget, you'll need to be very judicious about where you spend your money. Looking at the data in the example, it only shows ad performance for one month. As you accumulate data over time, you'll see trends that will enable you to make wiser decisions about the best places to advertise your business to drive your sales.

Response Rate

The response rate is just like the CTR, only it measures an off-line response to an advertisement.

To calculate the response rate for a magazine advertisement:

(# of responses) ÷ (circulation of magazine) = response rate

The obvious question is: How can I measure the response rate to an ad I placed in a magazine? A good way to do this is to include some sort of offer in the ad. This gives prospects a reason to respond to the ad so you can measure its effectiveness. You've often seen ads that tell customers to mention a certain code when calling in to take advantage of a special offer, or you've seen codes in small print on postcards that a company wants people to send in to receive a free gift. These codes tell marketers exactly which ad a prospect is responding to. By using different codes for each ad, you will be able to measure which ads have been most effective because you can tell where your responses are coming from. This will help you determine what kinds of offers are most effective in increasing sales and which outlets are the best places for you to advertise.

Cost Per Customer

Knowing the cost you are paying to acquire each new customer can help you determine which advertisements and promotions to do and which to avoid.

To calculate a promotion's cost per customer:

($ spent on promotion) ÷ (total # of new customer orders) = cost per customer

The money you have spent on a promotion includes advertising costs, mailing costs, or any other costs associated with trying to acquire new customers through this particular promotion. If your average order value (AOV) is $20, it would be unwise to regularly pay a $100 cost per customer. If, however, you sell products or services at a high price point, you may be able to afford to spend more to court new business.

Return on Investment (ROI)

This calculation is used to determine what kind of return you'll get on a marketing investment in your business. You can use this to measure your investments on promotional activities, to see if the promotions cost you money or made you money.

To calculate the ROI on a marketing program:

$$\frac{(\$\ \text{made from promotion}) - (\$\ \text{spent on promotion})}{(\$\ \text{spent on promotion})}$$

ROI is typically expressed as a percentage so, if you spent $1,000 on a promotion and made $1,500 from that promotion, your ROI would be 0.5 or 50%. The higher the return on your investment, the better.

Email Open Rate

Email marketing is a great way to build and maintain a relationship with your customers and, thanks to email marketing companies, it's easier than ever and very affordable. While it may feel nice to have a large number of people on your mailing list, email marketing companies typically charge based on how many subscribers you email. Rather than being concerned with only the *quantity* of subscribers on your list, it is important to be concerned with the *quality* of your list. A smaller number of well-targeted and interested customers and prospects is preferable to a huge list of people who have no intention to buy.

Your email marketing provides an effective way to stay in front of your audience and let them know about products, services, and promotions that may interest them. If they don't open your emails, however, they won't see your messages, which renders your email campaigns ineffectual. For this reason, it is important to measure your open rate so you know how many people are actually reading your emails. If people aren't opening your emails, the time and money you are spending on this activity are wasted.

To calculate your email open rate:

(# of opened emails) ÷ (# of emails delivered) = email open rate

By paying attention to which of your email subject lines have the highest open rates, you can learn what your customers respond to and tailor your subject lines accordingly. While subscribers would be very likely to open an email with the subject line: "Save 50% on your next purchase!" that doesn't mean you always have to be losing money to get subscribers to open your emails. Creative subject lines that communicate value to your customers can be just as effective. For example, a jewelry designer may find that the subject line: "Get this season's hottest styles" performs well with fashion-conscious consumers, without offering a discount.

While measuring email open rates is by no means a perfect science because opens aren't always reported accurately, for a variety of technical reasons, having some measurable information is certainly better than having none. It can still provide a way to observe trends and changes in customer behavior based on changes in your marketing.

Tracking Where You Sell the Most

If you sell your products at a number of different retail outlets, it is helpful to know which stores are bringing in the most sales. For example, if you sell t-shirts with your own original designs, you can easily monitor the percentage of stores selling your shirts.

Stores	**# of T-Shirts Sold**	**% of Total Orders**
Store A	26	26 sold ÷ 52 total = .5 or **50%**
Store B	17	17 sold ÷ 52 total = .327 or **33%**
Store C	9	9 sold ÷ 52 total = .173 or **17%**
Totals	**52**	**100%**

As you can see in the example, Store A sold the most shirts this past month. If this is a consistent trend, it presents an opportunity. Perhaps you could approach this store with new products that customers might also like. Wherever you see success, you can try to duplicate it to build your sales.

As I mentioned earlier, marketers measure anything and everything related to the effectiveness of promotions and sales. If these common formulas whet your appetite for tracking your marketing success, there are new books and websites coming out every day that can provide more in-depth detail about how to measure each and every aspect of your sales and promotion activities.

CHAPTER 23

The Importance of Marketing Data

Business Lessons From Reality TV

There have been some really informative reality shows that have offered interesting and entertaining insights on the workings of business. Among them are *Dragon's Den*, *Shark Tank*, and *The Apprentice*. While the intention of these programs has been more to entertain than teach, they still manage to highlight some common problems that can undermine the success of many businesses, particularly smaller ones.

In one episode of the UK version of *The Apprentice*, a women's team and a men's team were challenged to develop and present a toy concept and prototype to a major toy manufacturer. The team with the strongest product would win. The women's project manager led her team to defeat because she repeatedly chose to ignore marketing data and feedback.

The women's team ran a focus group to determine what types of products were most desired by the target market, which was a very wise thing to do. Consumer feedback clearly indicated that prospective consumers significantly preferred the team's toy robot over the team's card game. After a vote in which the women's team decided that the toy robot was the product that should be promoted, the project manager ignored all input and overruled the team's selection. She chose to promote the card game, which she had conceived. Why? Quite simply, her ego clouded her judgment. She preferred the card game because it was her idea.

When the project manager's card game was presented to a successful toy manufacturer, it received a less-than-enthusiastic response from experts in this industry. Despite even this indicator, the project manager maintained that her concept was superior. Not only did she cause her team to lose, she was "fired" from the show. Fortunately, this was only a TV show challenge but, had this been a business investing thousands, or even millions, in this project, the consequences could have been very serious.

Business decisions should be based primarily on logic and concrete data, not emotion.

Many in business fall victim to their own ego, but business decisions should be based primarily on logic and concrete data, not emotion. Certainly, there's room for some gut instinct, but that alone is insufficient for solid decision making. If all available evidence irrefutably supports a particular decision, it would be unwise to repeatedly ignore such strong facts.

At the end of the day, the opinion of prospective customers is the most important because they are the ones who will, hopefully, be purchasing your product or service. Be sure to listen to customers and prospects, and act accordingly. Even when you're not asking questions, customers and prospects are still talking. Whether they're telling you they love your website or that they think you have lousy customer service . . . listen. Your responses to their opinions may make the difference between profitable customer retention and expensive customer acquisition.

The Value of Research

Research can save you a tremendous amount of money and time. You don't necessarily need to hire an expensive research firm, you can simply do some investigation yourself to obtain the information you'll need to make smarter business decisions.

Research that you collect for the specific needs of your business is called **primary research**. It can be gathered through surveys, focus groups, or by observing customer behavior.

For example, if you want to know what percentage of the people at a local rock club live within a 20 mile radius of the club, you could have someone at the door ask patrons how far they have traveled as they enter the establishment.

Research that already exists because it was collected by another person or organization for their specific purposes is called **secondary research**. This can include information such as competitive intelligence, studies, surveys, and websites.

For example, perhaps you want to know what kinds of crafts are best-selling. You may come across a study of the industry that was conducted by an organization that serves the crafting industry. This could save you a tremendous amount of time and money. Why reinvent the wheel, when you can utilize data that was already collected by a reputable organization?

CHAPTER 24

Advertising

Advertising Versus Publicity

While free publicity is very valuable and has its place in any solid marketing plan, it is only one of many valuable components. Sending out press releases does not constitute a comprehensive promotion strategy. As you manage your own marketing plan, consider the role that paid advertising can play in how and where you get your message across.

Many entrepreneurs readily see the value of free publicity, yet the importance of advertising may not seem as obvious. Advertising is important, however, because, as an advertiser, you have more control over where your message appears, how frequently it is seen or heard, and what it says to your potential and existing customers. Marketers buy advertising because it works. Depending on how you design your advertising campaign, it can usually also be measured so you can determine which advertisements drive more sales for your business.

Targeting Ads

The best place to advertise is wherever your potential customers are likely to be. Your customers are out there, no matter how narrow your niche. Find out where they spend time and get your marketing messages in front of them, wherever they are. If they are an affluent demographic that listens to talk radio, then place ads there. If they are a young, hip demographic that spends a lot of time online, you may want to buy banner ads on the music websites they visit.

The biggest mistake I see creative entrepreneurs make, when purchasing ads, is blasting their messages out to a huge, untargeted audience. That is a surefire way to burn through the marketing budget without getting good results. Untargeted ads may never even be seen by the people most likely to buy from you, which won't result in increased sales. Targeting your advertising as finely as possible is a key to developing a successful advertising strategy.

Developing Effective Ads

Effective advertisements are clear and concise. Visual ads, such as magazine ads or online banner ads, can perform particularly well. As a creative person, you have the advantage of being able to come up with original and compelling ideas. Your natural talents can serve you well, as you design ad concepts.

When working on the visual aspect of ads, keep in mind that **negative space**, the space around your copy and graphics, helps readers to process the information you are communicating. In a culture with short attention spans, a clever visual ad can be immeasurably valuable. Don't feel the need to fill every bit of space with words or images. Less can most definitely be more because it gives your message more impact.

As you write your copy, be aware that shorter lines of text get better results than a solid paragraph because the negative space separating the text makes it easier for a reader to process. Since everyone's time is valuable and there is so much competition for the public's attention, it's important to get to the point up front, or you might lose people.

When designing your ads, keep in mind that a message that is immediately understood is the most effective. This is true, regardless of the type of media you use: print, online, TV, radio, etc.

During the Internet boom I worked for an online retailer. At this time shopping online was still a novelty, so to promote the website, I came up with a banner ad that simply showed the company's logo with the line "Shop in your pajamas." We placed numerous ads online and mine was one of our top-performing banners because it expressed a simple message in a simple way.

When designing advertisements, remember that people are bombarded by hundreds or thousands of ads every day. The average person is desensitized and can easily tune out advertising messages. In the few seconds that a person sees your ad, can you communicate a message that will either be quickly and readily understood or, at least, make someone want to slow down and learn more about what is being advertised?

Frequency of Advertising

It's important to not only get out your message, but to get it out over and over and over. Since you're so close to your business and see everything from close range, it may seem like you're repeating yourself and that your message will get less attention the more you get it out there. But the exact opposite is true. Because people are so adept at tuning out marketing messages, repetition of your message is extremely important.

The more people hear or see it, the more likely they will remember it.

An additional benefit of repetition is that you're letting people know that you are a serious businessperson, rather than some fly-by-night seller who may not be in business next month. An active ad campaign keeps your message in front of prospects and is reassuring to them.

Increasing Your Response Rate

It is not only critical to get your message out there, but also to get both prospective and existing customers who hear your message to either respond or buy from you. This is known as a **call to action**, and it provides the incentive some may need to take action on your marketing message sooner rather than later.

Advertisers do this all the time by urging people to "call now for special pricing" or by telling them that "this is a limited time offer" to give people a sense of urgency. By setting a deadline, those on the fence or potential procrastinators are motivated to act now. Sweetening the deal by offering a bonus with a purchase can be very effective, but be sure to include an expiration date so people have an incentive to buy today rather than put it off.

Where to Advertise

As you determine where your target market will most likely see your ads, you will have a variety of options in regard to where you can place your advertisements. More traditional places to advertise include newspapers, magazines, radio, television, and billboards. You can also buy ads online, including banner ads and contextual ads.

I have seen increasingly creative advertising methods in recent years, including ads on the floors of grocery stores and a restaurant that sold ad space on its drinking straws. Any space that many people will see may be considered as possible advertising space, whether it's a tangible space or space online.

CHAPTER 25

Using Publicity to Drive Sales

Why Publicity Matters

In my line of work, I meet many talented people who are struggling to build their businesses, despite offering high-quality products and services. They provide superior customer service and offer excellent value for the money so what's the problem? In many cases, it is simply down to not getting their message out to prospective customers.

Consumers can't buy a product if they don't know it exists. This presents a challenge to even the best small business owners and solo entrepreneurs. Amidst the constant marketing noise from TV, radio, point-of-purchase displays, newspapers, magazines, billboards, signs, and even video screens at gas station pumps, consumers are bombarded by multitudinous advertising messages each day. It is increasingly difficult to stand out from competitors, particularly if those competitors have large advertising budgets.

Consumers can't buy a product if they don't know it exists.

Advertising is an effective way to get out your marketing message, but it's also very expensive. Fortunately, developing a public relations (PR) strategy is a less expensive way to reach prospective customers to drive your sales and complement any advertising you do. By providing news and content to media outlets, you can get media exposure that will reach your prospects.

Getting press coverage is an important component of almost any successful marketing plan. Why is it so important? Certainly, being free doesn't hurt, but the value beyond that is that media coverage is perceived by the public as objective news, whether it actually is or not.

Consumers know that an ad has been purchased so the content it contains is only going to favorably promote the advertiser. In contrast, media coverage has more credibility because the individual or business being covered does not have control over the content, therefore it is seen as more accurate and balanced than advertisements. Additionally, people assume that, if you are receiving media coverage, you must be more successful and, thus, better than your competitors because only successful artists are interviewed by the media. This perception can be very advantageous for your business.

Interestingly, I have often seen my press releases appear in print media verbatim. While this isn't good from the standpoint of journalistic standards, as a marketer, I have no problem with it because, in those instances, I've just gotten my message out to the public exactly as I wanted it to be expressed.

The Power of PR

The reach and power of media coverage cannot be overstated. A number of years ago, a publicist I knew appeared on TV on an obscure local channel at an odd time of the day in the background of some B-roll footage. Though PR was her profession, even she was amazed by how many people caught that fleeting glimpse of her on television. Her phone had been ringing off the hook since it aired. She told me that was when she fully appreciated the power of television.

Media coverage transforms the way people view you and your business. It gives you credibility and positions you as a leading professional in your field. Because publicity is so powerful, many people want it.

Back when I started in PR, the media were far more likely to send out a reporter to cover a story. These days, media companies have suffered layoffs, just like every other company, so there are far fewer people working at these outlets and fewer reporters to cover the same amount of news. Media professionals are busier than ever so you really need to have a strong hook and get to the point.

When trying to come up with strong hooks, think about the kinds of headlines you see on the magazines found at the grocery store checkout. Those attention-grabbing headlines are written to interest shoppers enough to spur an impulse buy. Because journalists and producers know that those kinds of headlines work, they will respond favorably to them.

By crafting your press release headlines to sound like magazine headlines, you will have much greater success in getting publicity. Since TV shows, magazines, newspapers, and radio stations generally make most of their revenue from ad sales, they need stories that will give people a reason to stay tuned because the bigger their audience, the more they can charge for ads.

How to Get Publicity

As you can imagine, journalists, editors, and producers are inundated with press releases. Here are tips to improve your chances of getting the press coverage you want:

Focus your efforts toward publications and programs that appeal to your target audience.

For example, if you are promoting an interior design business, it wouldn't make sense to send a press release to a sports magazine. By sending your news to outlets that cater to your target demographic, you will greatly increase your chances of getting coverage.

Make sure your press releases provide real news and value to media outlets.

Their main concern is providing content that will interest their audiences so pitch your story ideas with their audiences in mind. It is important to remember that media outlets are not in business to promote your company. Will their viewers want to stay tuned after the commercial break to hear a story about the fact that you just redesigned the look of your office? If not, it's time to come up with a better story to pitch.

Journalists, editors, and producers have very tight deadlines.

These people don't have time to keep chasing sources for additional information and photos. Make sure you have supporting information and graphics or photos ready to send, before you even contact journalists. As soon as they request information, send it to them immediately. Also very important is to send materials in *exactly* the format that is requested. If one journalist wants you to copy and paste information into an email, while another wants a Microsoft Word attachment, respect their requests. If you are asked to send photos in a high-resolution TIFF format, don't send a low-resolution GIF. The easier you make it for journalists, the better your chances of getting coverage.

***Make sure your press release answers:* who, what, when, where, why, *and* how.**

Your first paragraph should contain the most important information so that, even if someone only read that, the general message of the press release would be clearly understood.

Work to build a positive relationship with the media.

By providing stories that have value to an audience and being easy to work with, you'll increase the chances that journalists will remember you the next time they need a quote for a story related to your area of expertise.

Developing an Ongoing Plan

One press release does not constitute a marketing plan. Countless times, I have been approached by people who fully expect that one or two press releases will have offers pouring in, including interviews with major network TV shows and multi-million-dollar sponsorships. They expect a couple of interviews to double their sales overnight. When this doesn't happen, they learn the hard way that getting media coverage is no substitute for a solid marketing plan.

Sure, appearing in the press is a wonderful way to promote your products and services, build your brand equity, and increase sales. There is a reason, however, that marketers talk about a "marketing mix" when discussing overall marketing plans. There are a number of very important factors that need to be considered and addressed, when launching into a marketing plan. Relying too heavily on only one component, such as publicity, means that your plan will be incomplete and, therefore, ineffective.

By incorporating publicity into a full mix that addresses all of the components in chapter 19, you can develop a stronger strategy that will be comprehensive. Publicity can play an important role in your plans, when you are also paying attention to the full spectrum of marketing vehicles at your disposal.

CHAPTER 26

How to Write a Press Release

Develop a Strong Pitch

Pitching to the media means that someone is contacting a journalist or producer with a story or show idea for consideration. The person pitching wants to be featured by the media outlet to get publicity. This is a worthwhile exchange because the person pitching can provide interesting content and information to the media and, in return, this person receives media coverage.

What would constitute a good pitch to the media? Developing an effective pitch is part art and part science. Certainly, you want your pitch to be timely and attractive to the media, but how can you do this?

First, think of something strong and current you can say about what you do. Having said this, it is also important to remember that this current news item should be of interest to people other than you. It should be something that people who don't know anything about you or your business would want to read about, hear on the radio, or see on television.

If I had a dime for every time a client wanted me to send out a press release about "urgent, breaking news" that their company has been in business for five years this month, I'd have . . . well, I'd probably have an extremely large pile of dimes, at the very least. My point is that the general public doesn't want to read stories about businesses managing to stay in business for another year. Would you want to read about that? Probably not.

Humans are hardwired for self-interest so they want to read about news and information that will benefit *them*. They want to find out about things that will save them money, protect their families, improve their health, or entertain them. Because of this, television programs, radio shows, newspapers, websites, magazines, etc. are looking for these types of stories that will attract an audience. These media outlets generally make their money through subscriptions, advertising, or a combination of both. If they fail to attract an audience, they will go out of business. So, you can increase your likelihood of getting press coverage, by working *with* these publications and combining your priorities with theirs.

Second, if there is a big national story in the news on which you can comment, that is another proven way to increase your chances of getting media coverage, especially in your local market. Local news stations love to have a local angle on a national story. If you can effectively tie your pitch into a national story, it is suddenly more appealing to your local media. Keep in mind that it should really be a good fit because, if it isn't, you could end up damaging your reputation with the media.

One of the first times I used this strategy was years ago when I was working in the cable television industry. At the time, the reputation of cable companies was very bad, after many years of poor customer service fueled by monopolistic arrogance. A comedy called *The Cable Guy* was about to be released in movie theaters nationwide, and the cable industry was buzzing with fear. Cable executives were afraid the movie would further harm the industry's already damaged image. In an effort to get out a positive message from the Philadelphia cable organization I represented, I used the national story of the release of the movie to pitch *The Philadelphia Inquirer* with my message of how the cable industry was working to improve its customer service. My plan worked like a charm, and I scored a very nice article for the organization.

How to Write a Press Release

When writing a press release, focus on the newsworthy elements of your message that will be most interesting to the media. Your first paragraph should contain the most important information, with the first sentence communicating as much of the *who*, *what*, *when*, *where*, *why*, and *how* of your message as possible without being cluttered or unclear. Any of these elements that don't comfortably fit into the first sentence can appear in the next sentence or two in the first paragraph of the press release.

Don't feel that you need to provide voluminous information in a single press release. People have a tendency to try to fit in far too many details, but it is wiser to keep the text of your press release brief and clear. I have measured the response rates to press releases I have sent out and found that a one-page press release gets a better response from the media than press releases that are two or more pages long.

You really only need to provide sufficient information to pique the interest of the reader. Believe me, when journalists and producers are interested, they will get in touch with you to schedule an interview or request more information.

What follows is an example of a typical press release. While there are some minor style variations between PR professionals, this is the format that I use.

[NOTE: For the purpose of example, the following press release uses fictional names for people, product lines, locations, organizations, and awards. Any resemblance to actual people, product lines, locations, organizations, and awards is coincidental.]

FOR IMMEDIATE RELEASE

Press Contact:
John Smith, Media Relations Director
[*phone number*]
[*email address*]
[*website*]

Local Jewelry Designer Offers Hollywood Glamour on a Budget

Philadelphia, PA—October 27, 2012—Today, Mary Jones announced that her new jewelry line, the Red Carpet Collection, will be launched on December 1st at her boutique on 7609 Carnival Avenue. This new line pays homage to the glamorous starlets of the Golden Age of Hollywood, by recreating their elegant style of jewelry in affordable pieces.

"I am thrilled to be bringing this new collection to the public," Jones enthused during a public announcement held this morning at her studio. "I believe that sophistication and luxury should not just be reserved for the very wealthy. Every woman deserves to look and feel like a star."

The launch event will be held from 9 a.m. to 9 p.m., with champagne and canapés being served from 3 p.m. to closing. Jones and her staff will be available to give customers personalized advice on how to achieve high-end style without breaking the bank.

About Mary Jones
Jones has been a professional jewelry designer in the Philadelphia area since 2005. Her work in both fine and costume jewelry has earned her recognition from major fashion and style magazines nationwide. Jones was the recipient of the ZXYZ Jewelry Design Award for the past two years.

###

CHAPTER 27

Seducing the Media

Be a Great First Date

Courting the media is much like dating. Too much too soon can scare off an attractive candidate so it's best to leave them wanting more.

Just imagine if you went on a first date with someone who immediately wanted to tell you his or her entire life story and was already making wedding plans, before you really got to know each other. You'd most likely run for the hills.

Instead, it's far better to present just the information that will interest the media. Give them exactly what they want, the way they want it. This will not only help you get great media coverage but, before you know it, your phone will be ringing without you even having to send out a press release.

Avoiding PR Pitfalls

It is not uncommon for people to think that there is nothing more to PR than sending out press releases, but this is not the case. A good PR person can refine the quest for publicity into a veritable art form. Successful PR campaigns involve all manner of communications and relationship building. It's all about who you know and who you get to know. Networking with media contacts is of paramount importance, as is staying in front of your contacts.

While the thought of schmoozing your way to success may sound very appealing, it is serious business and, if done improperly, can do far more harm to your business than good. There are many common mistakes that novices striving for media coverage commonly make. By avoiding these, you can significantly improve your chances of getting the media coverage you want.

Put yourself in their shoes

Over the years, I have noticed that the media are far less proactive than they were when I started working in marketing and PR. In their defense, I believe this is largely because the media industry has suffered significant layoffs, just like every other industry. What this means is that, if you get a TV producer or journalist on the phone, you are talking to someone who, most likely, has to cover a workload that was previously done by two or three people. For this reason, they are extremely busy and overworked.

With fewer employees to do the same amount of work, media outlets are often forced to use familiar formulas that have worked in the past. They are frequently looking for new angles on stories that are already out there, rather than proactively seeking out new stories. Once you know this, you can focus on what value you can bring to them. The goal is to deliver a story that they can easily plug into their show or publication to offer value and interesting content to their audience.

Imagine being a TV show producer. You get into work, and on your desk is a stack of press releases and packages containing promotional materials. You log into your email and see an interminable scroll of emails from publicists looking to get their clients on your show. Your voicemail is full of messages from more publicists, either pitching or following up on previous pitches. Literally, hundreds of people want your attention, and you haven't even had coffee yet. After hearing thousands of pitches from people promising that their angle is completely unique, anyone could become a bit jaded.

I always try to bear this in mind, when I contact journalists and producers. They really do work very hard on excruciatingly tight deadlines and are often pulled in many directions at once. When you contact them, just remember what they have to deal with. By making life easier on them, you are more likely to get press coverage and form critically important relationships that can help build your career.

When "free" can be a bad word

This is a common mistake, in which someone actually comes right out and asks a media outlet for free advertising. This is not a good idea because the vast majority of media outlets make a large portion of their income from advertising. By asking to get this for free, it comes across that you want to take something away from them. That rarely goes over well with anyone.

Instead, the approach should be that you want to *give* them something of value. Be clear as to exactly how your story would be interesting to their audience. To do this well, it is important to know who their audience is and be familiar with the style of the outlet. Is the audience made up of business professionals interested in economic news or teenagers who love fashion? Is the style of this particular outlet formal? Casual? Hip? Humorous? These factors should help you determine whether your story is a good fit for any particular media outlet.

Your **pitch** is the way you present your story idea to the media, in the hope that you will get press coverage. Pitching a lighthearted story about the art of making wreaths to a serious newsmagazine probably won't be very effective, but a story about how your wreath-making business increased sales by 150% by capitalizing on a new home décor trend might be. By meeting the needs of the media outlet you are pitching to, you can more likely meet your own publicity needs.

Brevity is a virtue

When approaching anyone in the media, it is important to remember that they are constantly being approached by people who are looking for press coverage. Because of this, they don't have time to hear every detail about what someone is promoting. You must get directly to the content value you can bring to them, in a manner that is quick, professional, and friendly.

I cannot overemphasize the importance of being concise. Before you contact anyone in the media, write down three brief points that you want to make. If you get to discuss even one of them, you're already doing well. Being able to clearly and concisely articulate the value of what you do is extremely important. Doing so demonstrates to a reporter or producer that you have a mastery of your subject matter and are more likely to perform well in an interview and give them a good story.

When you send written information to journalists and producers, be sure it is brief and clear. A great way to present information in a way that is easy for readers to process is to present it in bullet points. As I mentioned earlier, the longer the text, the lower the response rate.

Remember, you only get a few seconds of their attention, whether you are calling or sending a press release. If your message doesn't hook them immediately, you will lose that particular opportunity for media coverage.

Don't become a nuisance

While it can be very tempting to keep contacting a reporter or producer, to see if they have decided yet whether to do a story about what you're promoting, it is not a wise practice. Reporters, editors, and producers are very honest about whether they're interested in a story. They have their plans on the types of coverage they want to do, and they know what interests their respective audiences.

If they tell you they're not interested, hounding them certainly won't help. If they tell you they are interested and they'll get back to you, this is good news. When this happens, it is perfectly acceptable to ask for a ballpark idea of when they might consider using your story. At that point, it's fine to ask, "May I contact you in two or three weeks to follow up?" If it is okay, simply mark your calendar and wait until then. If you haven't heard anything by that time, it is then okay to get back in touch with that person.

When you follow up, begin your call or email by letting the person know that you are following up as you said you would. This contact, whether written or on the phone, should be very brief. Simply remind the person who you are, why you initially called, and that you are checking in on the status of the press release you sent. Trying to further sell your story or repitch at this stage can be counterproductive and, possibly, ruin your chances of getting coverage. Follow the lead of the media person, and base your responses on this person's reactions.

Being considerate in follow-up contacts can improve the possibility of future opportunities. Look at the transaction from the media person's point of view. You may not get your story printed this time but, if you are polite and professional, you just might get coverage for your next story. Remain focused and positive. Building publicity for your business is a process that will take time.

Losing the Gig

A client once asked me if it was possible to lose an interview opportunity, if a call from an interested producer didn't go well. The simple answer is yes. If a producer calls with interest in having you on as a guest, giving verbose answers and never getting to the point could very quickly cause the producer to lose interest. Treat the phone call as a sort of audition during which the producer can assess whether you'll be good in an interview. It is critical to make a positive impression right from the start. Know your talking points backward and forward, and be ready to give clear and brief answers to questions.

Handling Interviews

When you're being interviewed, imagine how concise you would be if you had to pay a great deal of money for each word you said. That would most likely tighten up your marketing message so it packed the biggest punch for the lowest price. Thinking of answers in that way can help you to see what is critical to your message and what can be eliminated.

Start paying close attention to interviews that you see on television or read in newspapers, magazines, or online. Take notice of the kinds of questions that are typically asked of people in your field. Are they general questions? Are the questions related to timely news events? Are they questions that require knowledge of specific facts and research, or are they more opinion oriented? Perhaps most importantly, how would you answer the very same questions in an interview?

Also, pay attention to the rhythm of interviews. There is a certain cadence to them, and an interview is almost like a dance. The interviewer leads, but there is give and take, and a good interview is very smooth. Notice that, typically, an interviewer asks a question and only expects a short answer so that another question can be asked.

The appropriate length of an answer depends on the media outlet. For example, if you're being interviewed on Fox News or CNN, a very brief answer is sufficient. If you're on an Oprah Winfrey special, however, longer answers are appropriate. Be sure to watch at least one episode of a show, before going on for an interview. It's wise to be familiar with the feel of the show so you're not walking in cold.

Likewise, pay attention to the interviewees and how they answer the questions. Observe the elements of interview answers that you like and note why. Also, take note of what doesn't come across well in an interview. Try to avoid those types of responses.

Everyone gets nervous for their first few interviews but, eventually, you'll become more comfortable as you refine your interview skills and your answers. To give yourself a stronger chance of being a good guest, try the following:

- Know what's going on in your field, such as new trends and developments
- Determine your talking points before the interview
- Be concise and articulate
- Act confident (even if you don't feel confident)
- Be open and friendly
- Remember to mention the project you're promoting

- Be flexible and willing to talk about issues that the interviewer brings up
- Speak at a volume and tone to match that of the interviewer

By being a good guest, you will increase your chances of being invited back to the same show and be more likely to appear on other shows. Media outlets watch what their competitors do and, if you're a good interviewee, you'll get calls from other producers.

CHAPTER 28

Joint Promotions

Getting Exposure to New Markets

Building your business takes time and money so try to find efficient ways to reach new customers in your target demographic wherever and whenever you can. One effective way to reach new prospects is to get exposure to the existing customers of businesses that are not your competitors, but are also targeting the same customers that you want. To do this, it is important to have a clear understanding of your target market.

How to Find Businesses for Joint Promotions

For example, if you're a woodworker who makes high-end, customized pieces, such as classic fireplace mantles, traditional floor-to-ceiling bookshelves, and sophisticated custom cabinetry for grand homes and estates, your target market would be in a very high income bracket in your local area. These customers would likely be purchasing other very expensive items for their homes. If you put together a list of the types of businesses that are also trying to sell to the same demographic, your list might look something like this:

- art galleries
- interior design firms
- specialty and custom lighting sellers
- high-end garden and home décor centers

- antique furniture stores
- stores that sell decorative rugs
- high-end furniture stores

Once you have a list of these types of businesses, divide them into two groups: *competitors* and *non-competitors*. It is important to note this difference because you should treat them differently. The list above would look like this under these two categories:

Competitors	**Non-Competitors**
antique furniture stores	art galleries
high-end furniture stores	interior design firms
	specialty & custom lighting sellers
	high-end garden & home décor centers
	stores that sell decorative rugs

For the next step, start with your list of non-competitors and, under each type of business, write down names of specific firms that you'd like to approach. You can write down businesses in your area or even national businesses, if you're looking to reach national customers. You can also write down websites that reach your target market. These websites can be either sellers or simply information providers that appeal to your potential customers.

An effective strategy is to target these non-competitors for joint marketing efforts that will benefit both you and them. They will probably be receptive, if the value to them is readily apparent. As long as a proposed joint marketing campaign isn't too expensive and doesn't require an inordinate amount of work on their part, they'll be much more likely to participate, if the venture will bring them more customers and more sales. Direct competitors, on the other hand, are going after the exact same market that you are targeting so, when dealing with them, it's best to keep your cards close to your vest.

Continuing with the woodworking example, the list of non-competitors might look like the following list.

[NOTE: For the purpose of example, the following list uses fictional names for businesses. Any resemblance to actual businesses is coincidental.]

Non-Competitors
art galleries
Taylor Fine Art Gallery - in town
Big City Modern Art Gallery - the largest in the area
interior design firms
Jones Interior Design - highly respected local business
website covering arts and lifestyle for the region
specialty and custom lighting sellers
Country Lighting - in town
Smith's Custom Light Fixtures - upscale business
high-end garden and home décor centers
Deluxe Garden Center - in town
Uptown Home Décor - biggest in the area
stores that sell decorative rugs
the area's largest high-end rug dealer

Once you have a solid list, think about what you could offer that would not only benefit your business, by exposing you to new prospects within your target market, but would also benefit the other business owner. Without some sort of significant benefit to the other business, there isn't good reason for that business to participate in a joint promotion.

Say the woodworker wants to reach the customers who frequent a local high-end garden and home décor center. A suggested promotion could be asking the owner of the home décor center to incorporate some sample pieces within the showroom displays to make them more attractive and drive sales of the store's existing stock. The woodworker could then have small signs noting that the items are for sale along with brochures available in the center for any interested customers. The promotion is free to both parties because neither has to buy additional products, and the appealing displays can increase sales for both sellers.

The same woodworker could even suggest a joint promotion with a local art gallery in which both parties could share the cost of wine and hors d'oeuvres for a gallery show that would incorporate some of the woodworker's pieces into attractive displays showing how beautiful the art would look in a customer's home. Both parties could promote the event separately to their own customers so both would get exposure to a new audience. This sort of promotion is relatively inexpensive and can be highly effective if executed well by both parties.

[NOTE: I wouldn't recommend sharing customer information with another business. In my professional experience, customers don't take kindly to having their information shared, rented, or sold. If the news of an event is coming directly from you, they generally see the communication as news that would interest them.]

Even better, the woodworker and the gallery owner could team up with a local restaurant that targets the same group of customers, and the restaurant owners could provide samples of their dishes to entice people to patronize their restaurant. That would create even more buzz because there would be yet another element added to the event. Additionally, the restaurant would promote the event to its customer base, providing a third group of customers within the same target market that would be added to the mix.

I have attended well-coordinated promotional events like this, and they have been hugely successful for all of the businesses involved. If you hold this type of promotional event, just remember to try to get contact information from interested prospects so you can communicate with them again for future marketing purposes.

CHAPTER 29

Networking That Works

The Problems With Untargeted Networking

When I went through the part of my career in which I endured the worst struggles and frustration, I was continually told to try networking. Everybody I knew dispensed the conventional wisdom of calling everyone you've known since second grade and tactfully asking them if they have any connections, or telling them about what you've been doing in business and what you're looking for, in case they come across anything, so they'll keep you in mind.

Instead of the brilliant results I was told to expect, I experienced resentment and irritation, despite my best efforts to be friendly and diplomatic. Why? Because this type of broad-based and untargeted networking isn't news. So many people know about it that when you reach out to people, they're likely to recoil, regardless of how friendly and professional your approach.

I was also passed the recommendation to network within my industry so I joined a major association for professionals in my field. Again, instead of great results, I found that I was, essentially, networking with my direct competitors. It's hardly surprising that this didn't produce profitable results. We were competing for the same work so there was no incentive for people to help each other.

Further, instead of gaining valuable information from the association, I was continually being bombarded with marketing materials promoting the association's courses in their certification program. It felt like little more than a campaign to simply strengthen and enrich the organization rather than its members. Disappointed, I cancelled my membership after a couple of years.

I still believed that networking could be a major key to success, but I didn't know where I'd been going wrong. The traditional networking methods people frequently recommended produced no results so clearly I needed to try something different.

I eventually discovered that instead of using a broad, untargeted approach, I needed to use a targeted approach that focused on other entrepreneurs at my level who were seeking to serve the same or similar demographic groups but weren't my direct competitors. In other words, we were all trying to reach similar prospects, yet were offering these prospective customers different products and services. This is similar to the approach mentioned in the previous chapter but, instead of specific promotional events, it involves being able to refer clients to each other on a regular basis.

The Benefits of Targeted Networking

As I sought new people to contact for networking opportunities, I used the following criteria to determine which individuals were a good fit. I was looking for entrepreneurs who were:

1) At approximately the same stage of business growth as I was
2) Trying to reach the same or similar types of prospective customers that I was trying to reach
3) Non-competitors

Why was this approach so successful? Because we could very effectively help each other. We were, essentially, in the same boat and facing the same challenges with, roughly, the same resources. We were empathetic toward each other and immediately recognized the mutually beneficial opportunities in such business relationships. In helping others, we could also help ourselves.

Trying to reach out to well-established people within your industry can be an exercise in frustration and a very inefficient use of time because, quite frankly, people at high levels rarely reach down the ladder to help others. Sure, you'll hear about rare stories in which an unknown person reaches out to an industry leader who actually gives them the time of day, thus gaining an instant ride up the ladder to success, but, in my experience, these cases are anomalies.

The vast majority of successful people I have encountered have risen to success through their own hard work and perseverance without the help of any successful benefactors. There will always be legendary tales of people who were inadvertently discovered and quickly rose to prominence, but waiting for such an occurrence is tantamount to using the lottery as a retirement plan.

The good news is that, once I started to engage in targeted networking, my business opportunities grew dramatically. I gained ground more efficiently, which freed up more time to do other activities that would help build my business. I learned that this specific type of networking was a key to growing my business. Through targeted networking, I gained more clients, without ever advertising my services. These clients, obtained through my network of fellow entrepreneurs, were some of the best clients I ever had. They knew exactly what I did, how I could help them become more profitable, and were ready to pay well for my services because they recognized the value I could deliver in helping them achieve their career goals.

Likewise, I sent well-qualified leads to those in my network to help them get more business and become more profitable. I also bought products and services from many of them because I valued what they had to offer. As we all helped each other, we all saw our businesses grow, and we reached our individual dreams together.

It's very important to remember that successful networking is constituted of relationships in which both parties contribute benefits. If you treat it as an all-take-and-no-give proposition, you will quickly find yourself without a network.

The benefits of *efficient* networking can get you closer to your professional goals, in much less time than untargeted networking. As you seek out networking opportunities, consider people who may work completely outside of your industry with whom you could create creative business opportunities.

For example, if you're a craftsperson who makes baskets for home storage and organizational use, you may want to network with interior designers in your area or even home organization consultants. If you're an acting coach, it might be wise to network with local theater directors and even casting agency managers to find mutually beneficial opportunities. For as many types of creative entrepreneurs that are out there, there are even more potential opportunities.

CHAPTER 30

Premium Items

How Premium Items Can Drive Sales

Premium items are items like mugs, t-shirts, magnets, pens, calendars, polo shirts, tote bags, mouse pads, and baseball caps that are customized with a company's logo and, often, with the company's contact information. These items can be used to increase the awareness of your brand and, ideally, keep the name of your business and your contact information close by when a customer is ready to place an order.

The items you give away as premiums should be items that people will actually keep and use so that your brand name is frequently in front of them. One of the best premium items I've ever received was a small, non-breakable mirror with a magnet on the back and the company's marketing message on the front. When these arrived at the company I worked for, everyone immediately put them up in their cubicles because they were useful. That company's name was then seen all over the office so it remained at the forefront of people's minds. Being the first name that comes to mind when a customer needs the products or services you offer can make a dramatic difference in your sales.

Choosing What Will Work Best for Your Business

Any premium item you choose should be appropriate for your target market. For example, if your target market is rock fans, then t-shirts would be appropriate but, if your target market is executives, then an embroidered golf shirt may be more appropriate.

The importance of professional-looking materials cannot be overstated.

Also, the amount of money you spend on the premium item should make sense in relation to the price of what you're selling. If, for example, your average order value is $35, then giving away thousands of premium items at a cost of $20 each (including the items, customization, and shipping) would be unwise. The cost of the premium needs to be justified by the kind of sales it can bring in.

The importance of professional-looking materials cannot be overstated. Don't put your name on cheap premium items. It would be better to not have them at all than to use cheap items. The last thing you want is for prospects and customers to associate your name or company name with the cheap pen they have that never writes properly.

A particular challenge for many entrepreneurs is that they often only need small quantities of customized premium items. Many companies only offer large quantities, which have low per-unit prices if you're ordering 5,000 but, if you only need 25, you're out of luck.

Fortunately, there are an increasing number of companies that offer small quantities of customized goods at reasonable prices. Since there are always new companies opening, an easy way to find what you're looking for is by searching online using appropriate keywords. If you aren't familiar with any companies that can customize items, I'm happy to share the names of companies I have worked with. You can find them on my website at www.makemoneybeingcreative.com.

CHAPTER 31

The Importance of Efficiency

Trying to Do It All Yourself

I often hear life coaches talk about people not succeeding because they need to give themselves "permission" to succeed. While I understand that what they mean is that people develop perceptions about their own lack of abilities or self-esteem over time, the best way to combat this is with knowledge and resources.

Typically, the challenge I see creative entrepreneurs wrestling with is that they have too much they need to do in too few hours. They are busy because they can't afford to pay for the kinds of resources that would speed up their success. They're trying to do all the work of running a business themselves. No one can be an expert at everything, but many entrepreneurs can't afford to hire professionals to handle the various aspects of their career that require focused work and attention.

Most creative people I meet who sincerely want to change their lives in order to live out their dreams are very hard-working people who are knocking themselves out in their efforts to achieve success. They're not afraid of success, they are desperate for it. They're doing everything within their power to attain it but often don't have all the tools they need.

Initially, many creative entrepreneurs start off by doing everything themselves, or they manage with the help of friends and family. This can certainly get the business up and running but, as the business begins to grow and more opportunities roll in, the workload can quickly become unmanageable, for even the hardest working entrepreneurs.

Once you get to this point, it is important to know when to handle a project yourself and when to hire someone else. It can be very difficult to let go and hand some responsibilities to others, but it can also be a very wise move.

When to Start Hiring

A question that I frequently get from my workshop attendees is: “When should I start hiring staff or consultants?” This is an excellent question that deserves thought and careful consideration. I have seen many new entrepreneurs begin hiring staff immediately, and I have also seen many try to do everything themselves, long after the point at which they should have hired someone to help.

There are a few important factors to consider in determining when you should hire someone. What tasks are you trying to accomplish to advance your business? Administrative tasks such as billing, mass marketing correspondence, response tracking, and taking general inquiry calls, are among the most burdensome for entrepreneurs and can drain excessive amounts of your time during which you could otherwise be performing more profitable work.

While a primary reason for entrepreneurs not hiring employees or consultants is simply the lack of funds, when the benefits outweigh the costs, the possibility becomes affordable and sensible. To find out if you have reached this point, simply examine the actual costs of you doing a particular task yourself versus hiring someone else to do it while you work on another aspect of your business.

For example, if you're able to earn $200 an hour doing the main activity of your business rather than administrative work, it's probably time to start looking for assistance. If you can pay an assistant $30 an hour to handle paperwork and calls while you're making $200 an hour creating your primary service, you're being more efficient and actually increasing the profitability of your business. Handling everything yourself is frequently how creative entrepreneurs start out but, at some point, this becomes detrimental to your ability to increase revenue.

As another example, if you need content for your website, but aren't comfortable writing articles yourself because it takes you endless hours to write just one article, it may be more cost effective to hire a professional writer who can do the job faster. It comes down to considering the cost of your time. If it takes you five hours to write an article, it might only take a professional writer two hours.

While there is an expense in hiring an expert, it's the fastest and best way to get great results.

While it might cost $200 to hire a writer, if you're able to spend the five hours you would have spent writing an article on creating a painting that will earn you $1000, you're still $800 ahead. If you write the article yourself, you just spent five hours of your time during which you earned $0. Suddenly, hiring a writer makes a whole lot of business sense because it frees you up to do activities that will bring in more revenue.

Another big drain on time is when an entrepreneur is trying to do a job that really requires an expert. A good example of this is website creation. I'll use myself as an example. When I started out, I used a web design service that was inexpensive and enabled me to quickly put up a website that looked reasonably professional and gave me an immediate online presence.

This was just what I needed, initially, but, as I developed my business, I needed something more professional to ensure that I was presenting a professional image in the marketplace. Additionally, as my business grew, my needs changed, and my original website was no longer meeting the needs of my business. I had a few choices:

1) Keep my existing website and try to make as many changes as I could myself

2) Spend endless hours trying to create a new website using information I could get from books and online

3) Hire a professional who specializes in creating websites built to the latest standards and constructed around the specific needs of my business

I chose the third option, and it turned out to be a very wise decision. While there is an expense in hiring an expert, it's the fastest and best way to get great results. If I had tried to put something together myself, with the help of a friend who knew just a bit more than I did about building a website, I'd have spent countless hours on a project that would most likely have provided substandard results, and I would have lost all those hours during which I could have been earning.

The smartest option was to hire a professional because it could help take my business to the next level. While it was a cost, it was also an investment that improved my professional image, while ultimately saving me money and time.

When I am looking to hire someone, I typically ask for recommendations from other entrepreneurs I know and respect. I also keep a lookout online for the type of expert I'm seeking. Search engines make finding other professionals easier than ever, and many experts have their own websites displaying their credentials and examples of their work.

CHAPTER 32

Are Customers Costing You Money?

Sometimes the Customer's Not Right for You

When you're starting a new business, you'll very likely feel grateful for each and every customer you can get. Once your business begins to grow, however, you'll start noticing buying trends as you accumulate historical data on your sales.

You'll also notice that, while some customers are very profitable, others can consume such an inordinate amount of your time that they are actually a drain on your business and are, in effect, costing you money. While you most likely don't want to be pushing away customers, not all transactions are healthy for the limited resources of your fledgling business.

Certainly, you don't want to do anything to harm the reputation of your business. However, sometimes, the best choice is to end an active business relationship with a customer who is impossible to satisfy and too taxing on your time. While every situation is different, so you should take all aspects into careful consideration, there is a solution that has worked well for me a number of times.

After sincere attempts to satisfy a customer, if that individual is clearly a high-maintenance type as a matter of policy rather than due to any failure on my part, I simply advise the client that, regrettably, I don't seem to be able to meet his or her needs, which is my primary goal. I gently explain that, in light of this, perhaps another business can meet the very specific requirements of this client.

Excellent customer service is genuinely very important to me but, let's be honest, occasionally, we all encounter some individuals who just like to be difficult, for no apparent reason. I'm not in business to soothe insecure egos, I'm in business to provide high-quality marketing services to clients.

Having such a potentially difficult conversation with a client requires great consideration and diplomacy. It is unwise to end a business relationship on bad terms. Sometimes, things just don't work out, and some clients and customers may not be a good fit for the products and services you offer, or vice versa.

That's okay. It's a big world out there so there's no reason for ill will or bad feelings. It's just business and needn't be taken personally. More often than not, however, you'll find that such customers frequently end up seeking alternatives on their own, so you won't need to "fire" a customer very often.

CHAPTER 33

Conclusion

Next Steps for Your Business

So now you have tools to use as you begin building your creative business. You can more accurately determine what resources you have and what you'll need. You can develop an image that suits both you and your customers. You've learned how to define your target market and reach the consumers within that market through effective public relations and advertising. You can build a solid foundation for your business and increase your revenue by streamlining your efforts. You know how to make improvements based on information gleaned from tracking your sales.

This is the fun part—diving right in and getting started! You can begin working toward achieving success in your dream job and creating the life you've always wanted.

Use this book as a reference guide to address various business issues as you face them. Be sure to keep good records and track your business finances so you always know exactly where you stand. Make wise spending decisions based on logic and accurate data, instead of emotion, so you'll spend judiciously. When in doubt, consult a financial professional.

To receive additional ideas that could help you to build your business, visit my website at www.raiaking.net and sign up for my free email newsletter. There, I not only share general marketing tips that can help creative entrepreneurs, I also answer questions I receive from people who are looking for tips that pertain to their specific type of business.

My other website is www.makemoneybeingcreative.com, where I feature interviews with creative entrepreneurs from various industries. They share how they built their businesses and increased their success.

Remember that by treating your customers well and offering them value, you can build a solid relationship with them. They may also become some of your most vocal advocates.

You can achieve success by employing the proven business principles that have been successful throughout history. The reason that traditional business principles have become traditional is because they work. That's why they have been used for so long.

When things get rough, and they will at times, believe in your talents and abilities, remain strong, and stay focused. Perhaps the best advice I can give you is to work hard, learn everything you can about your industry and business in general, and have fun! Now go out there and get 'em!

16587146R00125

Made in the USA
Charleston, SC
30 December 2012